Five-Minute Ministry

Five-Minute Ministry

*Ten Simple Principles for You to
Make a Difference*

Alan E. Nelson

Foreword by Carl F. George

BakerBooks

A Division of Baker Book House Co
Grand Rapids, Michigan 49516

© 1993 by Alan Nelson

Published by Baker Books
a division of Baker Book House Company
P.O. Box 6287, Grand Rapids, MI 49516-6287

Second printing, August 1994

Printed in the United States of America

Library of Congress Cataloging-in-Publication Data

Nelson, Alan.
    Five-minute ministry : ten simple principles for you to make a difference / Alan Nelson.
        p.   cm.
    ISBN 0-8010-6790-1
    1. Laity. 2. Priesthood, Universal. 3. Pastoral theology.
    I. Title.
BV4525.N45   1993
253—dc20   93-15177

This book is lovingly dedicated to my sons, who have taught me a lot about making the most of my minutes, and who continually minister God's love to me in everyday fashion.

Contents

Foreword

Concerned laypeople in many churches and in many more small groups are searching for practical help in the form of simple methods that will energize their meetings and help them reach their potential. Small group leaders and those of the clergy who train them are constantly in need of illustrations and ideas that can make them more effective in touching others. The suggestions Alan Nelson gives in this book will work, whether they are used by people concerned with how to conduct meetings or with how to stimulate the interest of friends or acquaintances who might be invited to take part.

I met Alan Nelson several years ago and was immediately struck with the clarity that characterized his appearance, speech, writing, and graphics. I felt that Alan was someone to watch. Not only was he an excellent communicator, he was also committed to organizing a new congregation. *Five-Minute Ministry* is evidence that under God's nurture Alan has become an exceptional toolmaker. Though hard to put down, and easily read in an evening, this is much more than a casual one-evening reader. The book describes a lifestyle for sharing the gospel message.

The reader uncovers the message of the book by listening in on conversations between laypersons in a church, in the setting of home group meetings. The group members search for ways to relate to one another and to extend the benefits of their group fellowship to outsiders. I found myself reading and rereading the narratives, trying to memorize the language that gave such fresh and helpful insights into relationship building.

Returning as Alan does again and again to exchanges that help us develop a sensitivity to the neediness we find around us, stimulated me to see the often missed potentials for touching the lives of others. I was challenged to open my eyes and get ready to reach out, even in the middle of a fully scheduled life, to take advantage of opportunities that present themselves for only a few minutes at a time. By linking suggestions into easily recallable groupings, Alan gave me tracks to roll on. I knew where I wanted to go and what could come next. Anxiety reduced, hope aroused, my sense of venturing into relational ministry with those I encountered was quickened.

Combining the motivational language and story form of author Og Mandino, well known for his popular business books, with the life principles and leadership formulas used by author Steven Covey, Alan has produced a ten-part design for helping laypersons become the fruitful witnesses they desire to be.

We are indebted to Alan Nelson for putting good ideas in user-friendly form. This is a toolbox that I will recommend to many.

Carl F. George
Diamond Bar, California

Introduction

Called to Be Ministers

All Christians are commissioned as a holy priest-hood that is to make a difference in the world. Ministry occurs when we demonstrate Jesus to others. Most ministry opportunities lie within fertile five-minute units throughout the course of our every-day lives.

Tom and Janet walked up the driveway of the house where the Bible study was to meet. The Malibu lights along the sidewalk guided them to the front door. A few months after moving to the community the couple had been invited by Ron, a co-worker of Tom's, to visit his church. Attending this church had now become a very enjoyable habit for Tom and Janet, a part of life they had done without for the first ten years of their marriage. Although they had both been raised in Christian homes, the churches to which their parents belonged seemed impractical and unrealistic, so they quit attending after they left home for college.

But things were different now. Although children, careers, a home of their own, and varied social activities kept Tom and Janet busy, they had found that a degree of success did not bring the expected levels of satisfaction. Their values had changed. And so had church life, at least life at their new church. Tom found himself looking forward to Sunday mornings, and he had suggested this Bible study to Janet. "If my old college buddies could see me now!" Tom said with a smile as he knocked on the door.

The door opened, and they were greeted by Ron's wife, Maryann, whom they had met at church. "Tom and Janet, it's great seeing you again. Come right on in," she said with a broad smile.

"Thank you. Hi, Maryann," Tom responded.

"We're glad to be here," Janet added. "I love your house."

"Thanks, we really enjoy it. Ron will be here in a minute. He's setting up more chairs," their hostess offered. "I think you've met most of the group. Make yourself at home."

Maryann led the way into a spacious living room filled with people. Some stood and others sat, chatting in a friendly manner, but nearly everyone greeted Tom and Janet warmly. The people at church and in this group seemed so friendly, so accepting and genuine—quite unlike the rest of the world—and this increased the excitement Tom and Janet felt about returning to their spiritual roots.

The evening began with some sharing of the week's events, a few prayer requests, and announcements about church activities. Tom looked across the room and saw someone who looked remotely familiar to him, so he leaned over and whispered to his friend Ron, "Who's that in the corner?"

Ron looked in that direction and smiled. "Around here we call him the Five-Minute Minister. He's our guest teacher for this new series we're doing, and he's also a divisional manager at our company," Ron whispered back. "You've probably seen him at work, if not at church."

"I thought he looked familiar," Tom responded. "What did you call him? The Five-Minute Minister? Why?"

Ron chuckled. "You'll see."

Just then, the man in the corner asked the group, "How many of you here think very often about what your life is about, why you do what you do, and how you could leave your mark in the world?"

"How about every Monday morning?" someone suggested. Several group members laughed in agreement.

"Well, you're not alone. One of the wisest persons who-ever lived tells us in Ecclesiastes, 'I undertook great projects. I built houses for myself and planted vineyards. I also owned more herds and flocks than anyone before me. I denied myself nothing my eyes desired; I refused my heart no pleasure. My heart took delight in all my work. Yet, when I surveyed all that my hands had done and what I had toiled to achieve, everything was meaningless, a chasing after the wind; noth-ing was gained under the sun.' Then he goes on to say, 'Now here is the conclusion of the matter, fear God and keep his commandments. For this is the whole duty of people.'

"I remember, as an adolescent, looking with my parents at a home they were considering buying. On the wall inside the front door of the small house hung a glass plaque that read, 'Only one life; so soon it will pass. Only what's done for Christ will last.' That slogan clearly addresses our search for mean-ing and purpose. However, once we got past the entryway, we saw rooms littered with cigarette butts, empty beer cans, clothes lying around, and a kitchen full of dirty dishes. That home is a little like our lives. We want to make a difference in the world, but we wind up cluttering our days with rou-tine tasks and essentially meaningless activities. I believe the only worthwhile thing we can do that will outlast us is what we do for Christ. That is what ministry is all about.

"In Exodus 19:5–6, God says, 'Now if you obey me fully and keep my covenant, then out of all nations you will be my treasured possession. Although the whole earth is mine, you will be for me a kingdom of priests and a holy nation.' God was not referring there to the Levite tribes, those designated as the official clergy of the day. He was telling the entire nation of Israel that they were to serve as ministers to the world. So, too, God has called all Christians—people of the New Testament covenant—to be priests in our society.

"For too many years, church pastors and staff members have received most of the joy and spiritual rewards that come from ministering to people. Since they have also shouldered the burdens and heartache that come with their calling, these professionals have a high burnout rate. But, as we have been studying, Paul tells us in I Corinthians 3:9 that we are all God's fellow workers—the fields where God grows his spiritual fruit. Someone once wrote, 'The laity are not *in* the church; they are not *for* the church; they don't do things *at* the church. They *are* the church.' Jesus has called us to be fishers of men, [Matt. 4:19]. We are to be the light [Matt. 5:14]. We are to be harvesters [Matt. 9:38]. Peter says, 'You also, like living stones, are being built into a spiritual house to be a holy priesthood, offering spiritual sacrifices acceptable to God through Jesus Christ. . . . You are a chosen people, a royal priesthood, a holy nation, a people belonging to God, that you may declare the praises of him who called you out of darkness into his wonderful light' [1 Peter 2:5, 9]. You see, on judgment day, there aren't going to be two lines for Christians, one for the laity and one for the clergy. All believers are called to be ministers, to make a difference with our Christianity."

A man sitting near the speaker commented, "I was raised as a Catholic, believing that there is a great difference between the people in the pews and the priest, who was considered holy and therefore distant from the rest of us. I see what you are saying, but I'm finding it difficult thinking of myself as a minister, much less a priest."

"I know what you mean," the Five-Minute Minister said. "I've attended Christian conferences where a person would introduce himself as John Doe, pastor of some community church in such-and-such city. Then he'd wait for me to respond in kind. I used to tell him my name and then add, 'I'm just a layman.' *Just* a layman? We laypeople often have such a low self-image as Christians, that it's no wonder we don't get more ministry done. Several years ago, a plastic surgeon named Maxwell Maltz realized that even after he surgically corrected his patients' deformities, they often continued to think of themselves as ugly. He discovered that people respond to life according to how they see themselves. But God sees us as a holy people. As long as we see ourselves as '*just* laymen,' we're going to have a hard time thinking and acting as if God can really use us.

"How we see ourselves affects what we achieve. Ministry starts by believing that God can work through us. While I was growing up, we used to have a bowl of artificial fruit on the table. It was beautiful, but you couldn't eat it. Because the fruit was wax, it had no nutritional value. We can do good deeds all day long, but unless God's Spirit is at work within us, those activities are about as effective as that fruit. Jesus says, 'I am the vine, you are the branches. Apart from me you can do nothing.' True faith is believing that God is in us to *do*, not just to be."

"Tonight you've been talking about all of us doing ministry," another man reviewed. "I, too, have been taught that ministry was the responsibility of pastors, preachers, and other trained professionals. This idea of nonprofessionals doing the work of the church sounds sort of like those people are getting off easy. That's what they're taught and paid to do, isn't it?"

"That's a great question," the Five-Minute Minister suggested. "For years and years, churches have taught that ministry is the duty and privilege of an elite few. But the Bible tells us that it is every Christian's obligation to use his or her

God-given gifts and abilities to do specific tasks and perform certain roles for his church."

"Then why have so many of us been taught that ministry was for the professionals? Where have we gotten the feeling that we're incompetent or at least not responsible for ministry?" another man questioned.

"Who knows for sure?" the Five-Minute Minister responded. "But I think there are three possible reasons why most Christians do not see themselves as ministers. The first reason is the clergy's reluctance to encourage this. There has always existed a certain elitism among the clergy. In the past, the local priest or preacher was often the only one in the community with a formal education. He therefore had a lot of social prestige and was sometimes considered to be second only to God in wisdom and authority. The idea of the priesthood of all believers might seem to downgrade a pastor's specialness, and superiority. Perhaps some felt threatened by having a layperson do ministry, and maybe even better ministry than they could perform. Still others did not want all the hassles involved in training and equipping people for the work. Often it seems easier to do a task yourself instead of putting up with someone else's possibly mediocre performance.

"I think another reason for a lack of a ministry self-image is biblical and theological ignorance. Certain dogmas and beliefs tend to be taught at the expense of others. The passages we looked at tonight have always been part of the Bible. None of us put them there. However, through tradition and selective editing, we've just not put much weight on teaching and explaining the concept that all of us are called as priests. But I think the third possible reason may be the most likely. That is, an unwillingness for laypeople to see themselves as ministers."

"Why would Christians avoid thinking of themselves as priests if the Bible tells us differently?" a woman inquired.

"Think about it," the Five-Minute Minister said. "We hire people to mow our yards, cut our hair, clean our clothes, fix our cars, care for our children, and prepare our tax returns. Why not pay a few professionals to do our spiritual service as well? We do it in other areas of our lives, and we think this absolves us from responsibility. It's much easier than worrying about ministry ourselves. Not only that, if we take seriously the idea that we are ministers, that could put a crimp in our lifestyle. Remember, we behave according to our self-image, so if we see ourselves as a priest or pastor, we would have to watch how we think and act more carefully. It is human nature to avoid accountability.

"For example, think what would it take to tarnish your concept of our pastor at First Church. What kind of movie, if you saw him coming out of the theater where it played, would make you say, 'My pastor went to see *that!*'? Or what sort of story would he tell, or joke would he laugh at, that would make you say, 'Pastors don't say those things and shouldn't laugh at such jokes?' We've designed our own set of double standards. The Bible says that those in leadership positions will be judged with great severity, but there is only one set of standards for Christians. We are to be a *holy* priesthood. God has called you to be the pastor of your office staff, the chaplain of your neighborhood, and the priest of your son's soccer team. If your self-image reflects that, your lifestyle will respond in a complementary manner."

These ideas seemed quite novel to Tom, so he jumped into the conversation. "Excuse me, I'm sort of new here, but I've got a question," he apologized.

"Hey, you're part of the group," the Five-Minute Minister said, smiling.

"Well, Janet and I have been attending First Church awhile," said Tom. "We were both raised as churchgoers, but you might say we took a long vacation from that. Anyway, if it's the job of every Christian to be a minister, then why do we need clergy?"

The Five-Minute Minister replied, "I guess we need to rethink the role of the professional church staff. I'm not pastor bashing, or even suggesting we do without formally trained personnel. But we need to think of the pastor of the church as a spiritual facilitator, not *the* minister. His or her primary job is to enable the rest of the church to do ministry. Although we often refer to clergy as 'those in full-time Christian service,' it is every Christian's job to serve Christ daily. Certain functions in the church require specialized talents or training or time-consuming work, and that's why we need a professional staff. But their basic responsibility is to train, equip, and motivate the rest of us to be ministers."

All Christians are called to do ministry.

"You mean the pastor is paid to get us to work," Tom said with a smile.

"That's one way of putting it," the Five-Minute Minister laughed.

"Well, how effective can we really be as ministers? I mean, I've never been to seminary. And Janet and I have not been in church for a long time, so we're pretty rusty on the Bible and theology. What in the world could we do?" Tom asked.

"Ministry occurs whenever you demonstrate Jesus to others," the Five-Minute Minister responded.

"That seems simple," Tom agreed. "But I was thinking more in the line of preaching a sermon or teaching a Bible study."

"That's ministry, too, but it is just one small example. Because most Christians maintain very limited parameters of ministry, they miss a multitude of ministry opportunities. For example, if you asked me what a light was, and I pointed to the ceiling fixture and to the lamp on that table, I would be correct. But if you then developed the idea that a light source is always small and round, and either hangs from the ceiling or sits under a shade on a table, you would go through everyday life missing street lights, headlights, traffic lights, candles, fluorescent office lights, flashlights, Christmas lights, and the sun—all because your concept of lights was too small.

Ministry is when you demonstrate Jesus to others.

"For too long, we have been led to believe that God has called only a few select people for his work. By believing this lie, we have missed out on the wonderful joy that comes from being used by God to make a difference in people's lives. The teaching about spiritual gifts during the last several years has greatly enlarged our concept of ministry. As a part of Christ's body, we each have a unique function, although most of us do not think of ourselves in that way most of the week. Can you imagine owning some business franchise that only opened its doors a few hours a week? That's not very good stewardship. The Bible says that our bodies are the temple of the Holy Spirit. In essence, we house God's Spirit. Now there are two kinds of houses: permanent residences and vacation cottages. A residence is where you sleep, eat, work, shower, play, watch TV, raise the kids, and so on. A vacation cottage is where you go for long weekends, holidays, or a specific week or two per year. A lot of us consider our lives as vacation homes for God, so that on Sunday mornings, at a weekly Bible study, and during an occasional mission project during the year, the Holy Spirit is directly residing in us. But God considers our bodies a *residence*, open for business twenty-four hours a day, seven days a week. Wherever we go, God is with us, and his power is available for ministry.

"Look at this another way. Can you imagine the owner or coach of a sports team, drafting players, giving them a uniform, and having them sit the bench, but never intending them to play the game? There are no second strings on God's team. We're all starters. Or imagine a company that employed a thousand people, but only utilized fifty to a hundred of them. 'Hey, just show up when you're supposed to. We don't expect you to do any work. We're just glad you're a part of the company.' That would be ridiculous. And since God is the greatest manager/owner who has ever existed, he would never waste precious resources like that."

Tom asked, "Well, aren't the well-known professional priests and preachers our role models for effective ministry?"

"Many are," the Five-Minute Minister replied, "but throughout history, many of the people who made a great impact for God were not traditional religious leaders. Moses was not from the tribe of Levi, the family of priests. Neither was David, and he wrote many of the psalms that still move us deeply. When Jesus picked his twelve disciples, he did not choose men from the religious community, but fishermen, tradesmen, even a tax collector. D. L. Moody was a shoe salesman whom God greatly used to influence thousands of people for Christ. In fact, you and I can open doors that may be closed to a pastor."

"What do you mean?" Tom inquired.

"Some of us have circles of influence and social contacts that a pastor could not reach because he or she would be as suspect as a high-pressure salesman. There were two boys trying to outdo each other. One boy said, 'My dad's a doctor. I can be sick for nothing!' The other boy said, 'So what? My dad's a pastor, and I can be good for nothing.'" The group laughed as the Five-Minute Minister continued with a grin: "Pastors are paid to be good, but we can be good for nothing. What I'm saying, of course, is that when we take a stand for Christ or try to demonstrate Jesus to others, it often makes a greater impact than when those who are expected to live by faith reveal God's love.

"Besides, professional ministers are very few, and the ministry field is giant-sized. Everyone is needed for the harvest. In the Book of Titus, Paul tells us to present the kind of example that will make the gospel of Christ 'attractive,' perhaps like the setting of a ring shows off a diamond. The Good News is the diamond, but we must make the story of Jesus appealing to people. If you strip the hubcaps and chrome off a new Cadillac, it won't seem beautiful to many people in the showroom, even though it is basically an excellent car. We need to attract people to the beauty of Christ by displaying it in our lives. Most nonbelievers are not rejecting true Christianity. They reject their *perceptions* of Christianity, which they have gleaned from those who model it inadequately. When we shine, we don't need to cram spirituality down people's throats. They will borrow it from us if they like what they see in us. Before we can share the Good News with people, *we* must be good news.

"Someone said, 'You can lead a horse to water, but you can't make him drink.' True, but you can give him salt. Matthew 5:13 says that we are salt. This means we are to make people thirsty for Christ. We are to be appetizers for the gospel. An appetizer is not intended to fill you up, but to whet the appetite, to get the digestive juices flowing so that you feel like saying, 'Bring on the main dish. I'm famished!'"

Several people chuckled as the Five-Minute Minister shouted his explanation in melodramatic form.

Tom continued with a summary: "So you're saying that I am called to be a sort of priest, a minister to the people at work and those I live around? Whew! That puts extra pressure on how I act and what I say."

"You're right," the Five-Minute Minister responded. "Again, many Christians avoid this idea because they do not want to be held responsible for modeling a Christ-like lifestyle around others, but when you start thinking of yourself as a minister, you become more accountable. The clergy often refer to being 'called' by God. Laity, too, have a 'vocation,' a word based on the Latin word meaning 'to vocalize,' to call. Thus, if we are to do God's will, we respond to God's call to do ministry with our own lives. That is also why we need to pray really hard before we make any major lifestyle decision. God places us in certain areas for specific purposes, to affect certain people for him. You see, lay ministry is recognizing God's call, not being recruited by man. It is discovering a gift and being equipped to use it, not being coaxed. Lay ministry is serving others as God's faithful stewards. The beauty of this calling is that society expects pastors to act and think in a certain way, but when housewives, businesspeople, and other laity act like Christ, it somehow makes the gospel more authentic."

Tom continued, "I'm not trying to be the proverbial devil's advocate here or hog the conversation, but who has time to do ministry these days? Between work, the kids, fixing up the house, commuting, and regular church activities, there are not enough hours each week to do ministry, even if one wanted to do it. Besides, I'd lose my job if I spent much time talking to people about Jesus, and quite frankly, I doubt many would want to listen to me."

Ron jumped into the conversation. "Go ahead, tell Tom why we call you the Five-Minute Minister."

The man in the corner laughed and looked down, as if embarrassed by the unique title. Then he shook his head and said with a smile, "I'm not sure who gave me that ridiculous name. I'm sure it is some sort of religious takeoff from the recent business series called the One-Minute Manager. I accept the nickname, silly as it is, because I believe in the concept of five-minute ministry, and I want everyone to know about it. The idea comes out of my very firm belief that every single one of us can make an eternal impact on those we meet, if we understand and respond to the key ministry opportunities that come our way daily."

"Tell me more," Tom prompted.

"Most Christians never consciously do ministry because they do not understand that God calls every believer in Christ to be a minister. They also have the mistaken idea that ministry is pretty much limited to preaching a sermon, or going to Africa to feed the hungry, or teaching Sunday school, or calling on the sick or shut-in. Furthermore, since many acts of ministry require significant allotments of time and effort, those of us who are busy commuting, working long hours, raising kids, washing clothes, maintaining the car and yard, often doubt we have the time or energy to do it. So we decide that ministry on an ongoing basis is not for us. We let the paid professionals take care of it and avoid the Scriptures that tell us anything to the contrary.

"Most of our ministry concepts focus on inconvenience. We think ministry will require us to drive to a specified location and set aside a predetermined time from our busy schedule. Some ministries do require that, but we're not apt to do very much if it seems bothersome. We've all been at a meeting where someone needed a ride home. At the end, you try to figure out where this person lives and who lives the closest. Someone will say, 'Hey, I live on that side of town. No problem!' We usually avoid giving someone a ride on a consistent basis if it is 'out of the way.' We are a convenience-oriented society, with open-all-hours stores, home-delivery food and cleaning services, television shopping, and mail-order catalogs. Wouldn't it be nice if you didn't have to 'go out of your way' to do a majority of your ministry? Can you imagine being able to serve God and make a difference with your Christianity while maintaining your normal schedule? I believe that God confronts us with opportunities for ministry on a daily basis. He knows where each of us is at any given time, and he consistently places in our paths people he wants us to influence for him in some way.

"Besides the convenience issue, I think a lot of people avoid ministry because they perceive it as too time-consuming. If we figure that ministry involves a three-hour church service, including getting ready and driving time, preparing a Sunday school lesson and delivering it, or putting in a two-hour music rehearsal, who can do much ministry? But I believe that most ministry opportunities require less than five minutes of effort. God gives us enough time each day to do what he wants us to do. When we undergo time stress, it is either because we are doing more than he wants us to do, or we are misusing the time we have. Tom, have you ever heard of the Pareto Principle?"

"I think so," Tom said. "You mean the 80/20 rule?"

"That's it. The 80/20 rule basically states that 80 percent of all sales come from 20 percent of the salesmen, and 20 percent of our activities result in 80 percent of our productivity. It's the natural law that says we need to focus on what is important if we are going to be effective."

"So what does that have to do with ministry?" Tom asked.

"I believe that 80 percent of ministry potential lies within five-minute opportunities. Most are foolish enough to believe that ministry is only the long, formal, ritualized events of the church. God has designed a majority of ministry to take place in simple, everyday situations where we can make an impact for Christ. Like the iceberg below the water, most ministry involves quiet and seemingly uneventful interactions with people we meet throughout the normal course of events. We are called to be the salt of the world, but anyone knows that you don't smother food in salt to make it tasty. A dash here, a sprinkle there, is really the key to delicious food. So, too, most of your effective ministry opportunities can take place in five-minute units. Jesus did much of his ministry in that brief length of time. Remember his conversation with the woman at the well or his blessing upon the children? There were also the times he healed the lame man by the pool of Bethesda, turned water into wine, and told Zacchaeus to come out of the tree to welcome him. Sometimes these five-minute encounters opened the doors for extended ministry, as when he called each of his disciples. But those longer ministry times came primarily as a result of building a foundation upon an effective five minutes of conversation."

"I'm starting to see your point," Tom said. "Please go on."

"Well, Jesus gave us the parable of the sower. There is good soil, fertile but uncultivated soil, and worthless rocky soil. Because every farmer knows that you cannot get the same productivity from each type of soil, he develops his best soil for the most important crops. It is crucial to realize that there are a few significant situations in each day that are favorable for ministry. These opportunities require only an awareness of them, so that we can respond quickly and effectively. Believe it or not, you can do more ministry by taking advantage of these five-minute units than in years of full-time ministry activity that is not personalized. Occasionally, you may need to apply a succession of five-minute units, but an amazing amount of ministry can take place in only a brief time if you are alert to the fertile conditions for making an impact for Christ."

"Whew! This is a revolutionary idea," Tom said. "You mean, I suppose, that God calls each of us to minister in our places of business, neighborhoods, and civic clubs, just like he calls certain people to pastor churches and be missionaries on foreign lands. And within these settings exist various five-minute ministry opportunities that we need to recognize and act upon."

"That's right," the Five-Minute Minister said. "We are all God's ambassadors in our own worlds. Our responsibility is no different from our pastor's. It is to do the will of God, which includes being his representatives at work, at home, and in the community. Therefore, we must learn to see where people are most likely to notice the difference that Christ has made in our lives. If we do this, we do not have to hard-sell the gospel or push the church. Others' interest will come naturally. Like nuggets of gold scattered across a field these opportunities arise sporadically. Granted, there may be more valuable ore underground that is worth mining, but we ought to start by picking up the nuggets on the surface. The problem is that many Christians do not recognize these prime times for ministry or are intimidated by the idea of sharing their faith at the office or in the neighborhood. But God would not call us to minister if he did not also equip us and provide opportunities for us to serve him by serving others."

"So what are these right conditions to do ministry?" Tom asked. "How do we know when to engage in five-minute ministry units?"

"I would be happy to introduce you to what I call the ten power principles of effective ministry. Since nearly all of them take less than five minutes to activate, you can do ministry every day, without going anywhere other than where your normal daily life takes you. I'll give you a call and we can arrange to get together and discuss this more," the Five-Minute Minister promised.

Most ministry opportunities lie within fertile five-minute-ministry units throughout the course of our everyday lives.

The evening concluded with refreshments and fellowship. Tom and Janet liked the people in Ron and Maryann's group. Tom was especially drawn to the Five-Minute Minister and his creative ideas for lay ministry, which seemed both innovative and practical. "I think we're really onto something,"

Tom whispered to Janet as they walked into the cool evening air. The stars twinkled brightly as Tom considered the idea that he was called to do ministry and could make time for it in his hectic schedule. "I wish someone had taught me this before," he admitted. "I think things are going to change in our lives."

For Reflection and Discussion

1. What are the common reasons given for why more Christians do not get involved in ministry?

2. How would you have responded to Tom's questions regarding the role of professional clergy and the expectations we project onto our pastors?

3. How would you define ministry (illustrate, list qualities, etc.)?

4. How does the increase in our time pressures affect our lifestyle as Christians?

5. *Read 1 Peter 2.* What does this have to say about our self-image as Christians. (Note: non-clergy are referred to as laypeople, not lay-Christians.)

1

The Power of Bridge Building

Staying in touch with people is crucial for ministry. We build and maintain bridges with others so that during times of felt need, we can cross those bridges and minister to them.

The Five-Minute Minister had invited Tom and Janet to his home for lunch following the worship service at church. After the meal, he led the couple into the den, which also appeared to serve as his home office. Their host sat in the swivel desk chair while Tom and Janet completed the triangle in matching wingback chairs.

"We really appreciate your invitation for lunch," Tom remarked.

"And the food and hospitality were wonderful," Janet added.

"Well, thank you," the Five-Minute Minister responded. "My wife is such a wonderful hostess. She spoils me too. Tom and Janet, the reason I invited you over today was to follow up on our conversation at the Bible study last week. You seemed really interested in understanding the concept of five-minute ministry."

"To be honest," Tom said, "Janet and I have talked about the idea several times and are very serious about our renewed commitment to God. If he wants us to be active in ministry, we want to know how to do it effectively. I'm intrigued about your idea that someone like me can make a difference in another person's life in five minutes or less."

The Five-Minute Minister, at ease, chuckled and leaned back in his chair. "Tom, I never meant to imply that there is some secret formula for changing a person's life in only a few minutes. Although it's not as easy as it sounds, I'm sold on the idea that most ministry takes place in common, everyday situations. These opportunities arise whenever you are around people, but they require recognition and a simple response that takes one to five minutes to perform. Everyone is time-conscious these days. We're used to ATM's, microwaves, fax machines, cellular phones, teleconferencing, and fast-acting computers. So if I could show you how to let God use you to change people's lives in five minutes you would want to know, wouldn't you?" he asked.

"We sure would," Janet answered, as Tom nodded in agreement.

"Great. Now let's start learning the ten power principles that will explain how you can make those brief ministry units count. The first principle is the power of building bridges."

"What's that?" Tom asked.

"It's the idea that staying in touch with people is not only good for friendships and your business networking, it is crucial for effective ministry."

"Sounds like a takeoff on the phone company's slogan— reach out and touch someone," Janet giggled.

"You're not far off base," the Five-Minute Minister smiled in response. "I used to live on a farm in Iowa. On our farm was a dirt road that led to one of our fields. On this road was a small bridge that crossed a stream. The road was maintained by the county transportation agency and needed to be checked periodically for safety reasons. If the bridge was not inspected and maintained properly, it would fall apart and become dangerous. Relationships need maintenance as well, so that we can walk over into others' lives to do ministry when it is needed.

"The society we live in is fragmented in many ways. Relatives are scattered across the country. Families are dispersed among work, school, leisure activities, and commuting. People have more diverse roles as individuals than ever before. In my case, I'm a manager, a husband, a father, a Little League coach, a church board member, a teacher, and a PTA member. Each role has different requirements. Most of us have little time to develop friendships, but amidst this social desert, anyone can make a significant impact if he or she simply keeps in touch with people."

"But doesn't that take time?" Tom asked.

"Everything worthwhile takes time," the Five-Minute Minister agreed, "but it takes a lot less time than you think. For example, I have found that one of the most effective tools for bridge building is Postcard Power. Look." He opened the top drawer of his desk and pulled out a stack of prestamped postcards. "For just a few pennies, the United States Postal Service will pick up your personal message and hand-deliver it across the street or across the world. During the time someone puts you on hold on the phone, or you're waiting for your kids to get ready for school, or you've got five minutes between meetings, you can write two or three post-cards that will minister to other people. I keep the addresses of people with whom I want to build and maintain bridges in my desk and briefcase here, at my office, and even in my car. You can use an address book, the new electronic Rolodex cards, or just scraps of paper. I often have labels copied and just peel one off and attach it to a card. People do not mind as long as the message is personalized."

"Do people respond to this well?" Tom asked.

"Think about it. You're inundated with flyers and junk mail every day. It seems like everyone is asking for money or trying to sell you something. People usually have one of two responses when they get the mail. They either open the per-sonal letters first and trash the rest, or they quickly go through the bulk-rate materials and hold the personal notes for last, so they can savor them, sort of like saving them for dessert."

"That's true," Janet chuckled. "We sure do that."

"I've been to people's homes or offices several weeks after I've sent them a note and seen my card of congratulations or affirmation on the refrigerator or bulletin board, or even used as a bookmark. Tom, how does it make you feel when someone cares enough to drop you a note after meeting you, just to let you know they are thinking about you?"

"It makes me feel good. Sometimes I'll read it two or three times. It's sort of a pick-me-up in my day," Tom confessed.

"Exactly," the Five-Minute Minister smiled. "Another technique I use to build bridges is what I call Fax Fellow-ship." Tom and Janet grinned at the term. "The fax is a won-derful piece of technology, sort of a combination letter, telegram, and phone call. You might do the formal kind with a cover sheet and a nicely typed letter, but I often will hand-write a note, 'Hope you're having a good day,' or send a joke or cartoon that made me think about the other person. A friend of mine is an avid golfer, so when I see a comic strip of Charlie Brown learning to golf, I'll cut it out, paste it on a piece of paper, sign my name, and fax it to my friend. The beauty of the fax is that it is quick—you don't have to engage anyone over the phone, and the other person can read it at his leisure, just like the mail. It is inexpensive and takes under five minutes. We keep in touch with some of the missionaries we support in Africa this way. Instead of being thousands of miles apart, we are only a few minutes and a couple dollars away."

"That is a great idea," Janet affirmed. "It's a shame that with all our communications technology, we don't care enough to keep in touch that way."

"You hit the nail on the head, Janet. The key is caring. When you send a card, a letter, or a fax, you are saying that you care. It is a way of being present, even when you're miles away.

"The third bridge-building technique is the Telephone Touch," the Five-Minute Minister shared. "You can always use the fax or postcard idea, but the time-tested and most efficient way to maintain your bridges is with a brief phone call. There is nothing wrong with a long phone call, of course, but if you plan up front to keep it short and sweet, people never mind being interrupted. Just call them up and say, 'Hi, Susan, I was just thinking about you and wanted to tell you that I hope you have a good day,' or something to that effect. You don't have to talk in detail about the weather, or the business trip, or whatever. Just the fact that you called says three things. Number one, it shows that you were thinking about them and that their life means enough to you that you ponder their presence. Number two, it shows that you not only thought about them but were willing to put your thoughts into action. Most people do not follow through on their emotions. The third thing it does is acknowledge a person's existence. How many times a day do we get put down, challenged, beat up emotionally, or confronted?"

"A lot," Tom sighed. "I guess we can always use a word of support or encouragement."

"Tom is really good on the phone," Janet said, "but I feel awkward talking that way."

> *We build and maintain bridges with people so that during times of felt need, we are able to cross the bridge in order to minister.*

"Then you can stick to Postcard Power and Fax Fellowship, which are less personally demanding," suggested their host. "However, one of the nice things with our current technology is that there are many ways to use the phone without actually engaging the other person directly. Most people today have phone machines. Remember when the first one came out a few years ago? Many of the people who once vowed never to have one of those impersonal answering devices have broken down, purchased one, and now see them as a necessity. Sometimes I am glad when I call and get a taped answer, because it guarantees that I can keep my message the length I want. Some people have electronic mailboxes where I can leave a message, or I might leave a message with a secretary or receptionist if the person I want to reach is at a meeting. It will be simple and affirming, and it is nice to see a little pink telephone slip that does not say 'Please return call.' It means I am not asking anything burdensome but just dialed to say hello."

The Five-Minute Minister leaned back in his chair. Tom and Janet seemed to be thinking about his ideas. They seemed so simple. If this was a way to minister, maybe ministry was not that difficult after all!

"What do you say in these bridge-building times?" Janet asked. "I mean, we all know people who just call to talk your ear off, or write long letters, because they have nothing better to do. What excuse do you give to call or write?"

"Sometimes you may want to spend time on a letter or making a lengthy call to a personal friend or family member, but the five-minute strategy is just to maintain or build a simple bridge, not a mansion. That's why the proper technique is to keep it short and sweet. Otherwise, you end up procrastinating. You can find many reasons to build bridges. I will often send a note after I have had a meeting with someone, just letting the person know I enjoyed our time together."

"You mean you'll even drop a note if you bought someone's lunch?" Tom laughed.

"That may sound like overkill," the Five-Minute Minister admitted, "but it says that spending time with the other person was important. Sometimes I will just say hello, or include a joke or story. One of the best times for that is when I think of a person whom I have not seen for a while, like a small-group attender, a person at church, or just a friend from the racquet club. A note or call lets such people know that you have not forgotten them. It keeps the bridge maintained, even if it is not being used a lot at the time."

Tom looked at four small boxes on the desk and pointed to them. "Are those part of your bridge-building toolbox?"

The Five-Minute Minister smiled and then handed one of the boxes to Tom and said, "This just may be my most functional tool, as handy as the pair of pliers in my garage. Thank-you notes. Remember the story in the Bible about the ten lepers who came to Jesus and were healed? They all ran away, excited about their transformation, but only one returned to thank him. Jesus asked a rhetorical question: 'Weren't there ten of you? Why is it that only one returned to give thanks?' Jesus had just changed the lives of people who previously could not work or even live with their friends and family. Yet only one expressed his gratitude. I'm afraid that more and more, we are living in a thankless society. That is why thank-you notes are such great bridge-builders. They make a real impact because so few people use them well. I probably go through a box of these a week, and I supply them for all of my division people as well. I want our employees to have the reputation of being thankful. That attitude will get you further, and get you remembered, more than talent or looks or education will."

"If you go through a box of thank-you notes each week, what do you write them about?" Janet inquired. "And how do you find the time?"

"To be honest, that's only an average figure. Some weeks I will only send out three or four. Or I may sit down and write out dozens at a time. The thing to remember is not to spend a lot of time on writing them. Merely jot down three or four sentences or even a few words and then get it on its way. If an action becomes a chore, you might not do it very often. In five minutes, I can write a half-dozen notes."

"That's amazing," Janet said.

"Now, to answer your question of what to write about, look for detailed items to say thank you for, not just the obvious things. Of course, if someone takes you out to eat, or gives you a gift, or goes out of the way to serve you, send a note right away. But also send a note when someone does something promptly and with excellence, even when it is among that person's responsibilities."

Tom interrupted, "But why do you say thanks for things people are *supposed* to do, or what they are paid to do?"

The Five-Minute Minister smiled. "We expect a paycheck or official recognition when we agree to do a certain job or accept a responsibility. But we do not *expect* a thank-you note or applause. Gratitude is sort of dessert, a pleasant surprise. By delivering the unexpected, we make an impact that may be the first step in being able to minister to a person. A lot of what's involved in this power principle is what we might call pre-ministry. It is paving the road and building the bridge, so that at the appropriate time, you can use the bridge for more serious ministry."

"We do need to work on that," Janet admitted.

"I'll add," the Five-Minute Minister continued, "that one of the downfalls of being good at this is that some people begin to expect it. Therefore, when you stop writing thank-you notes for whatever reason, they may wonder if anything is wrong. But those situations are few, and compared to the masses who don't care enough to build bridges in this way, you will have emerged as a true minister."

Power Principle #1:

Build and maintain bridges with people via Postcard Power, Fax Fellowship, and Telephone Touches to lay the groundwork for ministry.

For Reflection and Discussion

1. Why is keeping in touch such a powerful tool for ministry?

2. Brainstorm and make a list of creative ways of keeping in touch with people.

3. Make a list of people with whom you could build and maintain bridges. Beside each name, list the "excuse" you could use to contact them.

4. Can you think of examples where someone impressed you by keeping in touch?

5. *Read Galatians 1:1–5; Ephesians 1:1–2; Philippians 1:1–6; Colossians 1:1–6.* What do these passages have in common? (Think of how Paul maintained his bridges.)

2

The Power of Initiating Interest

Priming the pump means initiating the first step in building a relationship.

"Can you tell us about another power principle of five-minute ministry?" Tom asked. "I really liked the first one."

"Sure," the Five-Minute Minister responded, "I like your eagerness."

"Wait, may I borrow a pen and paper?" Janet requested. "We need to get some of these ideas down in writing so we don't forget them."

"You've got it." Their host opened a desk drawer and handed both Janet and Tom some paper and a pen.

"Thanks," they responded.

"The second principle for five-minute ministry is what I refer to as the power of initiating interest. Think about it—nearly every friendship you have ever had has come about because one of you initiated a contact of some type. It might have been at school, during a club meeting, or before or after a church service, but today's best friends were yesterday's strangers. That's an important thing to remember, for two reasons. The first is that some people refrain from showing interest in strangers because they are shy or nervous, or they just refuse to get involved in others' lives. However, they fail to realize that they already have experience in this area or else they would never have developed any friends or business contacts. We all have used this principle in many ways.

"The second reason it is important to see that initiating interest is at the root of all our relationships is that we never know when we are being given the opportunity to make a friend. Most best friends did not seem like best-friend material when we first met them. Friends tend to grow on each other. The side effect of this ministry principle is that you can gain a lot of personal satisfaction and even professional networking with this simple five-minute technique."

"How does this strategy work?" Tom asked.

"The analogy I want to use here is the old water pump, the kind with the handle and spout that was used to get water from a well." The Five-Minute Minister gestured the motions of pumping.

"We know," Tom smiled.

"Good, I didn't want to seem too old! Well, when a pump is not used for a while, the leathers inside the shaft, which bring the water to the surface, become dry. Therefore, you have to pour some water down the shaft to relax the leathers. This is called priming the pump. You have to put a little water in to get a lot out. Opportunities to prime the ministry pump occur when you wait in lines at stores, pump gas, deal with a waitress or manager at your local restaurant, take your clothes to the cleaners, see new neighbors move in, watch your kids play soccer beside other parents—and the list goes on. Almost every time you are in a setting with a stranger, you have the opportunity to grab the handle and start pumping, but the other person's interest level usually needs a little priming."

"Whenever I get into situations like that at a grocery store, I'm not sure what to say," Janet admitted. "I think that's easier for some people."

"It's true," the Five-Minute Minister said, "that certain personality types are more comfortable with this than others. But all of us can initiate interest in our own way. If you are basically an introvert, your approach would be more quiet and low-key, less bold and energetic, but you will still be able to affect many people that way."

"What do you mean?" Janet asked.

"Think about it. Just as you have a distinctive temperament, so do the people in whom you initiate interest. Although you don't know much about the strangers you meet, some of them will be more open to a gentle approach than to the approach of a bolder, more aggressive personality. The issue here is not *whether* you should initiate interest, but rather how you do it. The best way to do it is to be yourself. And that doesn't mean doing nothing. Just feeling natural will give you a lot of confidence."

"I see what you mean," Janet acknowledged.

"Can you give me some specifics or ideas as to how you go about initiating interest in other people?" Tom inquired.

"Certainly," the Five-Minute Minister responded. "The best summary I can think of is based on using the letters in the word SALT. The Bible says we are the salt of the earth, so it's an easy outline to remember. S stands for Say Something. Over 90 percent of our population lives on less than 5 percent of our country's land mass. That means that most of us are urban in our orientation. We are getting more and more used to having people all around us. The bad thing about this is that because we get so used to seeing a lot of people in a short amount of time, we tend to avoid getting involved in their lives. We learn to set psychological boundaries, so we can actually be bumping up against someone in line but never engage the person emotionally. In the Iowa farmland where I grew up, whenever you met someone on the road, you would wave, nod your head 'hello,' or make some gesture to acknowledge the other person. Because you didn't see a lot of people, even strangers became somewhat special, so you initiated interest. Rural people have generally been considered very hospitable and friendly. To be honest, I don't think that's necessarily so. It's just that due to the less frequent interaction with people, they may make more effort to communicate with those they meet.

Priming the pump means initiating the first step in building a relationship.

"People in the city are perceived to be cold and aloof. But think about it. If we waved to everyone we saw and initiated contact with each person who crossed our path, we would go crazy. We couldn't do it, so, we tend to allow a certain anonymity. However, we make a mistake if we perceive this emotional distancing as disinterest. You see, the good side of having so many people in such small areas is that our opportunities for ministry are abundant. They are all around us.

"The power of initiating interest is based on the idea that it takes very little to let people around you know that you are friendly and recognize their importance. When you are surrounded by a lot of people in one place, there is a subtle feeling that you don't count very much as an individual. It's the old supply-and-demand principle. If you have a lot of something, pens in your desk, for example, you think nothing of loaning them out or of keeping them here and there. But if you have only a few, you take care of them more because each one is more valuable to you. Everyone wants to feel valued and special. When you initiate interest in another person, most people will let down their psychological guard and respond to your acknowledging their existence."

"I know what you mean," Janet affirmed. "A lot of times when I'm waiting at the check-out in the grocery store, I'll just look around or read one of the magazines in the rack. But occasionally I'll stir up conversation with someone in line. It's almost like pushing a magic button, and a complete stranger next to me will smile and talk to me."

Tom nodded confirmation.

"That's what I mean," the Five-Minute Minister said. "One reason we avoid initiating interest in others is that we're not sure of what to say. The S for Say Something means to say whatever you want, as long as it in some way initiates interest. You can smile and say 'hello,' and then comment on the length of the line or food prices or traffic or any one of a myriad of things."

"So it isn't important what you talk about?" Tom asked.

"Basically, no. Anything works. But the best thing is to find common ground as quickly as possible. Tom, when you and Janet met, you began a long process of finding out what each other was like. You asked questions and listened. The goal at the beginning of your relationship was to discover your areas of mutual interest. It is on that basis that we decide to increase or decrease our connections with people. It also helps us determine which direction we should proceed in a relationship. When we introduce two people to each other, how do we usually do it? We usually try to link them with something they have in common. 'Both of you moved here from the Midwest,' or 'John has a finance background, too,' or 'I think Mary also has two young children,' or 'You both play tennis.'

"When you have nothing else to talk about with a stranger, you will probably talk about the weather: 'I heard it's sup-

posed to rain this weekend.'—'I know, but we need the mois-
ture.' Because everyone shares the effects of weather, it's
the lowest common denominator we all experience."

Tom laughed. "Do you mean we're really scraping the bottom when we talk about the weather?"

The Five-Minute Minister chuckled. "Let's just say it's
probably the safest single topic of conversation. But the Say
Something technique is primarily just to break the ice, to
prime the pump.

"The A in our acronym stands for Ask Questions. The question should not be threatening, but something that is somewhat generic and friendly. It will vary from situation to situation, because if you are a man talking to a woman, you might
be perceived as more of a threat than if two women are talking. All the while, you're looking for an element of common-
ality on which you can build more interest and conversation.
If you're in a grocery store, you might ask about the price of
the tomatoes that you notice in the person's cart. If you're at
a school PTA meeting, you can ask what grades the person's
children are in and how long they have been attending the
school. You can ask new neighbors where they are moving
from. Or you can ask simple personal questions like how long
they have lived in the area, what they do for a living, or something that might bring up things you have in common."

"What if the person doesn't respond?" Janet asked.

"The purpose of asking low-key questions is to let the others know you acknowledge them and want to be friendly.
The other person may be having a bad day and not want to
be bothered, or may just be bashful, but most people will
respond to your priming the pump.

"The next principle opens up most people. The L stands
for Listen. Few people do that these days. Everyone has an
agenda, an opinion, and something to say, so some of your
best ministry is simple listening. Look the person in the eyes,
nod your head, smile, laugh if appropriate—just respond!

The initial moments with a person we do not know tend to be somewhat awkward for everyone, yet we all know we want and need attention from others. Listening is the key, because it will help you very quickly decide on what you should say next, what tangent to pick up, and what hidden needs the other person may be expressing."

"So you're saying that all of this can be done in just a few moments," Tom commented.

"A few moments is all most of us have to initiate interest. That's why five-minute units are crucial to ministry as a whole. If we are ineffective in making the most of brief, prime situations to influence other people, we will never establish a basis for doing more involved ministry down the road. Obviously, I'm going into some detail here in order to explain this power principle and provide some illustrations, but realistically, initiating interest usually happens in five minutes or less."

"What's the *T* of SALT stand for?" Tom asked.

"The *T* stands for Turn the Conversation to Something Deeper. There is some latitude into what I mean by 'something deeper,' but I basically mean you should try to find a point of need in the other person. Some of this has to do with the next power principle I'd like to talk about, but the point is that everyone has places of felt need in their lives. Everyone has a soft spot. Finding it is the key for effective ministry."

"I don't mean to disagree," Tom interrupted, "but I've met some people who don't appear to have any felt needs. They seem so cold, so put together and distant."

"Some people may seem that way at first," the Five-Minute Minister admitted, "but as you get to know more people, you will find that everyone has soft spots that can be targeted for ministry. I remember a time when my wife and I were taking a vacation in Europe on a group bus tour. The couple of people who smoked sat in the back where the smoking section was. Since the rest of us did not smoke, our tour guide set up a seat-rotation system so that everyone had only a couple of days near the smokers. One older woman in that section seemed so cold and hostile that my wife and I had pegged her as unreachable. When it was our turn to sit directly in front of the smoking section, we were not surprised that no one talked to her. At one stop, we finally decided to say 'hello' to this prickly lady and prime the pump. When we asked if she was married, she told us a gut-wrenching story of how she and her husband had booked this tour a year before and then he died suddenly. She decided to go on the trip anyway, but it was obvious that the woman was in great emotional pain. My wife and I felt like worms for prejudging her. After we got back on the bus, we talked at length with her and became her best friends during the remainder of the trip. Why? Because we discovered her soft spot. We realized that this cold, crabby lady was really just in pain. When we discovered what her hurt was, we were free to minister to her more effectively."

"I guess we must misunderstand a lot of people," Janet admitted. "It is so easy to just write off those who appear aloof and unpleasant."

"That is very true," the Five-Minute Minister responded. "Ironically, those are the people who need ministry most."

"But aren't you taking a risk whenever you express interest in others?" Tom asked.

"You are. No doubt about it. You are becoming vulnerable to a certain degree, whenever you initiate contact. The other person might reject you, but taking risks, even if they are small, is a part of ministry. It involves steps of faith. A law of physics says that an object at rest will tend to remain at rest, and an object in motion will tend to remain in motion. Initiating interest takes more emotional energy because you are moving something at rest—a relationship with a stranger—but once you get it going, it often moves by itself. In fact, you may see such a strong positive response from other people that *they* begin initiating questions.

"I think I should explain a little more about looking for deeper issues. Because everyone has a soft spot, and because your goal is to find common ground, try to get your discussion beyond just a customary greeting. Effective ministry needs to go beyond merely a smile. In my analogy of priming the pump, it took both the pouring of water into the shaft and then the initial pumping to loosen the leathers and bring water to the surface. Turning the conversation to deeper issues is the pumping process. Your intention, though unrushed, is to find out where you can build something of meaning."

"I think you're losing me on this one," Janet shared.

"For example," the Five-Minute Minister suggested, "you're at a check-out stand and by asking questions you discover that the woman in front of you just moved to the community from another state. She also implied that it is hard to make friends in new communities. Ah, she shared with you a soft spot, a feeling of loneliness and insecurity. The chances are high, you figure, that you will never see this woman again. Therefore, you turn the topic to something helpful. You say, 'I felt that same way when we moved here three years ago. But I've really made some good friends through a church I found here.' That statement turns the conversation from moving, to loneliness, to a possible solution, namely a spiritual answer. The woman may respond with interest and ask you to tell her more. Or she may just close up. Her reaction will let you know whether you are invited to share more, or to retreat toward a less threatening topic."

"I think I understand," Janet said. "You're saying that my comments depend partly upon whether I will see this person again. If we will probably never meet again, I can risk more and focus on spiritual things like inviting her to our church. If the chances are high that we can meet again, I

resort to more friendship-building conversation so that I will
know how to approach her in the future."

"You've got it," the Five-Minute Minister affirmed.

"But what if you never do get to spiritual topics?" Tom
asked. "I mean, I get turned off by people preaching at me.
I don't feel good about doing it either."

"That's where you may misunderstand my point, Tom.
Although five-minute encounters rarely allow for deeply spiritual lessons, they cultivate opportunities down the road for
yourself or for someone else. You see, everyone we meet has
some type of opinion or attitude about God. It is not a question of, 'Are you for him or against him?' Rather, all of us
come to know God through a series of small decisions. It is
a process of taking incremental steps."

Janet and Tom's host reached into his desk and pulled out
a one-foot ruler. "Now, let's just say that the eight-inch mark
on this ruler is the place where a person makes a decision
to ask Christ into his or her life. You and I are between inches
eight and twelve. But most of the people we meet will be
somewhere between inches one and eight. By finding out a
little about a person, we get an estimate of where he or she
is on that line. Sometimes, you will initiate interest in people
who are already good Christians. At other times, you will
establish contact with people who are atheists. You don't
deal with an atheist the same as you do with a fellow believer.
You have to go much slower and build up trust. But by the
very fact that you are initiating interest, most people will
open the door and let you learn more about them."

"That makes so much sense," Tom replied, "and it helps
me look at sharing my faith in a new way. I sort of got the idea
I wasn't really much good at witnessing to other people unless
they prayed or walked to the front of the church afterwards."

"Evangelism, in its purest sense, is merely moving someone closer to the twelve-inch mark on the ruler, full acceptance of the Good News," the Five-Minute Minister

explained. "Evangelism beyond the eight-inch mark is often referred to as discipleship. In the big picture, God is using many people and many situations to work in the lives of others. We are only held responsible for doing our part. Sometimes we meet people who are ripe for the harvest talked about in the Bible. They are ready to be picked. When we meet such people, it means that there were a lot of other workers before us who planted the seed, watered it, and cultivated the soil. But it also means that unless we do our part along the way, many people will not move toward a relationship with God at all."

Tom and Janet were quiet for a few moments as they made some notes and thought about their host's ideas.

"Can you give us some more tips on finding common ground in various settings?" Janet inquired.

"Sure. For example, if you see neighbors moving in, you can drop by with a plate of chocolate chip cookies and a six-pack of cold soft drinks. A five-minute visit would be all you need to introduce yourself and initiate interest. Some people today go for years living beside neighbors whom they never get to know. If your child is on a soccer or baseball team, you could offer to have the players and their parents over to your house for a picnic. When you are at the park with your preschooler, you can ask another parent there about raising young children. At work, you can start a conversation by inquiring what job the person has, or how long he's been with the company, and what he did before this job. There are as many interest-initiating ideas as there are people. The key is doing something to prime the pump."

Power Principle #2:

Initiate interest in other people to prime the pump for ministry opportunities.

For Reflection and Discussion

1. List some everyday settings where you could initiate interest among strangers.

2. What are some things that keep us from initiating
   interest in others?

3. How did you meet and get to know your close friends?

4. What are some suitable introductory things to say
   when priming the pump (besides the weather,
   although that's not bad)?

5. *Read John 4:7–26:* How did Jesus initiate interest
   in the woman at the well? What were the results?

3

The Power of Open Windows

An open window is an emotional interest point in a person's life that suggests an opportunity for ministry.

Janet put her hand gently on her husband's shoulder and said, "Tom, we need to let our hosts enjoy the rest of their afternoon."

The Five-Minute Minister looked at his watch and responded, "Don't worry about us. We're both happy I can share some of these things we've learned."

Tom said, "Well, if it's okay, I would like to hear the next one of the ten power principles of five-minute ministry."

"It's not just okay, it's great," their host laughed. "The third principle is what I call the power of open windows."

"What is that?" Tom inquired.

"Remember how, in the first principle, the power of bridge building, I used the analogy of the bridge and suggested some ways of staying in touch—building a bridge and keeping it maintained?" Tom and Janet nodded. "And the second power principle was illustrated by a water pump. Well, the illustration to remember here is the concept of an open window. Awhile back I played a video game with my son at an arcade. The theme focused on a paper boy whose job was to deliver newspapers to the homes in a neighborhood. My task as the player was to toss a newspaper through an open door or window. There were obstacles to avoid and also, the doors and windows would only open up periodically. The challenge was to throw it when they were open. A similar analogy can be found in miniature golfing. There always seems to be one or two holes through a windmill, so that you have to time your strokes strategically and wait until the rotating blades are past the alley where the golf ball needs to go. Otherwise, the ball gets blocked and knocked away."

"What's that got to do with ministry?" Janet asked.

"In real life, we all have periods of open windows when we are receptive to ministry and the Good News. This means that if you try to minister to a person at any given time, he or she may or may not welcome your outreach. But if you understand that there are specific times and areas that make a person particularly responsive and sensitive to ministry, you will not only be more effective in getting through to another person, but you will not experience the rejection or coolness we often receive when the window is closed."

"What sorts of issues are involved here?" Tom asked.

"I think it is best to put open windows into two categories," the Five-Minute Minister explained. "There are time-sensitive windows, and topic-sensitive windows. Time-related windows represent significant moments that are oriented to a specific event or period of time in a person's life. Fixed time windows are things like birthdays, anniversaries, weddings, the anniversary of the loss of a loved one, and the like. By 'fixed' I mean that pretty much every year, certain dates are remembered. Unfixed time windows are mainly traumatic but continuing events such as sickness, divorce, the loss of a job, an accident, or family conflicts, which tend to come and go on no particular schedule. You'll learn more about these bad times later. But when you discover such situations, you can be certain that a person is more apt to be open for contact and receptive to ministry during these times.

"The other category is topical windows. These refer to the typically ongoing areas of interest in a person's life. Let's try another analogy. Those of us who live in two-story homes know that there are times we open the downstairs windows, though we generally close them at night for security reasons. On the other hand, the upstairs windows are more apt to be left open at night because there is little chance of someone getting in that way. Now, without stretching the illustration too far, time windows are more like downstairs windows in that they are based on significant moments that tend to be open for a limited period. Topical windows are more like second-story windows. They tend to be open more often. These windows may be points of interest like hobbies, social concerns, sports teams, family interests, and past hurts. Even people who seem closed and aloof have interests that they are open to talk about. At work, some of our managers complain about employees who seem apathetic and unmotivated. But the same woman who sits hour after hour in silence at her desk will smile and talk willingly when you bring up the subject of her grandchild. Or the man who seems so unmotivated about selling turns into a bundle of enthusiasm when you ask him about his hobby of cycling."

"Okay, I think I understand the concepts of windows, time-oriented, and topic-oriented," Janet said. "But how do you find a window in a person's life, and what do you do with it? Where does the five-minute ministry come into play?"

"Since you realize what these open windows are and that everyone has these windows, you must first of all find them. So, you need to survey people. For example, remember when you and Tom came to our Bible study last week? Someone handed you an interest profile. On that sheet you wrote down your birthdays, anniversaries, hobbies, and other information about yourselves."

"I remember that," Tom responded, "and I thought it was interesting that the church wanted to get to know us."

"The reason for this is that it gives us some idea of at least a few of your open windows. All the people in my office and in our Bible study, along with their children, will receive a birthday and anniversary card from me each year," the Five-Minute Minister explained. "Just like the Postcard Power idea, I keep a record of names and addresses and special dates in their lives. When we remember significant dates, we enter a level of caring that says, 'Your life means enough to me that I celebrate with you on these special days.' I purchase several boxes of cards at a time, and it only takes a few moments to personalize, address, and mail a card. Yet, you've ministered to this person."

"It seems so simple when you look at it that way," Janet smiled. "What are the other open windows you mentioned besides birthdays and anniversaries?"

"You already know the two categories of windows: time and topical. But there are two types of responses. We celebrate wins, and we mourn losses. In essence, we offer praise for the positives and nurture for the negatives. Wins include things like birthdays, anniversaries, graduations, hobbies, and personal achievements. Losses include death, divorce, sickness, career setbacks, and family problems. It's a simple strategy—celebrate and mourn with others—but when you invest the few minutes it takes to acknowledge significant moments, you've learned an important lesson on ministry effectiveness."

"Can you give us some more ideas on how you celebrate and mourn with other people?" Tom inquired.

An open window is an emotional interest point in a person's life, through which you may do ministry.

"Sure," the Five-Minute Minister responded. "During our Bible study this week, John shared a prayer request about his family's financial struggle and the potential loss of his job. The next day, I shot off a little note to him in the mail that said I was thinking about him in my prayers, and I encouraged him to give me a call if he wanted to talk. John is facing a negative, so my response is nurturing. It communicates concern. Here's another example. Last week I was walking by my administrative assistant's office. There on her bulletin board was a new picture of her son with a soccer trophy. While I was in the grocery store with my family the next day, I happened to notice a sports magazine on soccer. I purchased it, attached a Post-it note about giving it to her rising soccer star, and laid it on her desk the next morning. You would have thought I sent her a dozen long-stemmed roses! She was elated and really seemed touched that I would care. It cost me only three dollars and took less than five minutes to do the whole act, but I scored a hit. You see, we're so conditioned to believe that ministry is making a home run. Just as most games are won by singles and getting on base, not homers, most ministry takes place by making effective small hits.

"Let me give you one more example. Our next-door neighbor is into local politics. About a month ago, I was reading the newspaper and saw an article about him with his picture. Though I'm sure he saw it and probably purchased some extra papers to send to Mom and all, I cut out my copy, clipped on a note to say I was impressed with his involvement—'Keep up the good work'—and I stuffed it into an envelope and put it on his front door. The next time I saw him driving by, he stopped his car in front of our house and expressed his thanks. It's the little things that make a big difference."

"It sure is simple," Tom sighed. "I guess there's really no excuse for us not doing things like that."

"How do you find out what another person's open windows are?" Janet inquired, "I mean besides the obvious questions like asking birthdates and anniversaries?"

"That's a good question," the Five-Minute Minister affirmed. "Janet, I think we're talking about an attitude. When you develop a mind-set of doing this kind of ministry, you just start seeing opportunities all around you. It's sort of like when you buy a certain model of car, all of a sudden you see cars just like yours in traffic. The best way to start developing this mind-set is to open up your eyes and ears. Look at a person's desk, car, or home. The artifacts we use to decorate, and the things we surround ourselves with, reveal a lot about our interests. A simple thing like a favorite type of pen can give you an idea of something to get that person when you're in a stationery store. Look for pictures of significant people, cartoons, quotes, books, music, or announcements around a person's desk. If you see certain equipment in someone's garage, or you notice them going to an event wearing a type of sports clothing, there's a clue. You can also pick up ideas by talking to them. If they seem happy, ask why. If they seem sad, ask why, or at least offer to listen. 'I'm thinking of you' cards are great if you're not sure what is going on in a person's life. By applying the principle of initiating interest, you can learn a lot about a person's open windows. <u>When you learn something new about a person, write it down and remember it</u>."

"You've made these ideas sound so exciting, but we really do need to be going," Janet said as she stood. "You have given us a wonderful afternoon."

"Thanks," Tom said, shaking hands with their host. "All of this is very new to us, and yet it seems so practical. I mean, we can do these things easily. I had no idea that ministry could be so simple and so much around us every day. I would love to find out about the other seven power principles that you talked about."

"Well, I'm sure we can work that out," the Five-Minute Minister suggested, as they walked toward the front door. "Tom, you and Janet are wonderful people. God can use you greatly when you start doing this type of ministry. I'll be excited to hear how it goes."

As Tom and Janet gave their thanks to the Five-Minute Minister and his wife, they realized that their new friends seemed so wise, so fulfilled in life. There certainly must be something special about using these ministry principles. Tom and Janet felt eager to get started.

Power Principle #3:

Every person has time and topical windows through which he or she will be receptive to ministry contact.

For Reflection and Discussion

1. List various time windows and topical windows in your life.

2. Discuss past open-window opportunities (conversations, current events) when ministry could have taken place (at work, church, family gatherings, or community events).

3. Why do you think ministry is more effective when a person's emotional windows are open?

4. List people to whom you could minister right now by celebrating wins or mourning losses.

5. *Read Matthew 4:18–20; Luke 15:3–7; John 15:1–8; Romans 9:19–23.* What do these passages have in common? How do they pertain to the ministry concept of open windows?

4

The Power of Acceptance

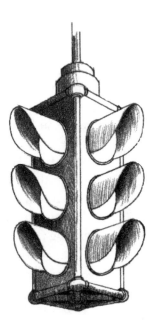

The green light of acceptance can signal the start of a relationship conducive to effective ministry, but it is vital not to confuse acceptance of a person with approval of a behavior or attitude that violates our principles.

Tom could not remember a time in his life when he felt more alive and excited. These days, the birds seemed to sing louder and the sun shone brighter. Surely it had something to do with this idea of five-minute ministry, because he was finding something each day to anticipate. Although he had always enjoyed his job, his family, and his friends, there was a new sharp edge on his life. His former routine had begun to wear thin, but now the concept of seeing everyday situations as a ministry environment gave everything new meaning. Unlike so many of his mid-life peers, Tom was finding a purpose for putting in the time and playing the various "games" one has to play to get by in life. And he wasn't just "getting by" anymore. He was doing more than climbing the corporate ladder and providing for his family. Tom felt alive to the daily possibilities of actually being used by God to change, at least in little ways, the lives of people who came across his path.

"Hi, Tom. How are you doing?" Ron asked, as he walked through the door of the restaurant where the two men had planned to meet for lunch.

"Just great! Things are looking up," Tom said with a smile, standing from his seat in the waiting area.

The two friends greeted each other and followed the hostess to a table.

"How's Janet and your little ones?" Ron inquired.

"They're doing better than ever. In fact, I was just thinking before you got here how much we are enjoying our growth in the church, and especially this concept of making our lives into a ministry," Tom responded.

"That's great! I knew you'd love the idea of five-minute ministry," Ron laughed.

"I know. It all sounds so sensible and simple, Ron, but it makes all the difference in understanding what our role is to be as Christians—what God expects us to do. I just don't know why no one told us about this sooner. We grew up going to church, and my concept of ministry had pretty much been limited to the pastor and a few retired saints. Now I see things differently."

"That's right," Ron affirmed. "The Five-Minute Minister told me he got together with you a couple of weeks ago. It sounds like you've started implementing some of the power principles he shared with you."

"Janet and I started that very afternoon," Tom replied. "We went home and sent thank-you notes to him and his wife, and to you and Maryann for the Bible study."

"Yes, we appreciated that," Ron injected.

"We maintained our bridges with several of the people at the office, on the kids' soccer team, and even in our small group. Look." Tom pulled a stack of prestamped postcards out of his suit jacket and laughed. "I'm hooked."

"That's wonderful," Ron responded.

"That's not all. While visiting the park with the children, I primed the pump with a man who just moved into the area. He works for our competitor, and I found out that we grew up in the same state. The funny thing is that we've seen each other a few times at the same park, but before meeting the Five-Minute Minister, I just sort of greeted this man and said no more. Now I'm becoming aware that God brings people into my life so I can make ministry contact with them."

"I know what you mean," Ron added. "We lived beside some neighbors for a few years before we actually got to know their names and interests and had them over for dinner. I was embarrassed it took me so long to understand that it's not just chance that people move across the country to the house next door. Humanly, you think it's just a good taste in neighborhoods or they got a deal on the house, but God has more in mind."

"That's true. Oh, and that's not all," Tom continued. "Janet found an open window for ministry last week when we saw an 'it's a girl' banner outside a house down the block. We hadn't yet met these neighbors, but Janet stopped in with some fresh cookies to congratulate them, and you would have thought they had won the lottery. The woman's mother was not able to come and help out, so Janet took them dinner a couple of times, and I think they're going to visit our church in a week or two. I mean, although everyone we've reached out to isn't a Christian yet, it's exciting to see the progress."

Ron chuckled. "Remember, ministry isn't just getting people to accept Christ. It's demonstrating Jesus to them.

Sometimes they end up coming to church and becoming a Christian. Sometimes they reject you altogether. Each ministry contact is an end in itself, and many lead to more and deeper opportunities like the one you mentioned."

"I'd like to find out more," Tom said. "The Five-Minute Minister mentioned ten power principles, but we haven't been able to get together since our first meeting to learn more than three. That's sort of why I wanted to have lunch today, to see if you could fill me in on some others."

Ron laughed again. "I thought you'd never ask! The Five-Minute Minister asked me if I would follow up with you. He got Maryann and me going on this approach to ministry a few years ago. It has made all the difference in our lives spiritually. If you remember, that's how you and Janet ended up back at church, because of our contact at work."

Tom smiled. "Why, you five-minute-minister you! I never even thought about that before. By George, it *does* work!" Both men laughed.

"Okay," Ron continued. "Let me give you another power principle for doing five-minute ministry. Here we use a green traffic light to symbolize the power of acceptance. The idea is very simple, but it is crucial if you want to establish a ministry relationship with another person. It is the basis for pretty much all loving relationships, and bottom line, that's what ministry is all about. The power of acceptance is primarily most effective when it is utilized during moments when you are tempted to reject another person for something he says or does, or for an attitude he exhibits. In psychology there is a saying: 'The I-am is related to the I-can.' In essence, how we perceive ourselves will determine what we attempt to achieve in life. In reverse, what we achieve and how we behave is often tough to separate from how we see ourselves. Therefore, when you communicate rejection of a person's actions, you run the risk of having that person think you reject him as an individual.

"Good parents learn that they must carefully separate the behavior from the child. They communicate this as: 'You are a good boy, but you've done a bad thing, Johnny.' In a similar fashion, we must learn to separate a person's value, whether sinner or saint, from the morality of his or her behavior or attitude. When we confuse the two, we are likely to alienate ourselves from people without even knowing what we are doing. Or, if we do know what we are doing, we sometimes figure that there is no way to take a stand for what is spiritually right, and at the same time maintain a ministry relationship with those who do not see things our way."

"Can you show me how this works?" Tom asked.

Ron leaned back as he responded, "The power of acceptance works in both old and new relationships. For example, when the guy ahead of you at the store is unshaven, has straggly hair, and seems unconcerned about your time pressure, you can give him either a red light of rejection or a green light of acceptance. The way we respond to people in the first few moments of meeting them makes a big difference in the quality and extent of a potential relationship."

"That makes a lot of sense," Tom agreed.

It is vital not to confuse acceptance of a person with approval of a behavior or attitude.

"First impressions are very important, and the signals we send to people will usually set the conditions for where that relationship will go. When you meet a new person, he or she carries around an invisible scorecard. Likewise, you have an imaginary grading pen, with which you draw either a smiling face or a scowl," Ron explained, illustrating his point in the air, using his finger as a pen. "The smiling face means you accept them—you give the relationship a green light.

We all like green lights because they allow us to proceed at will, but red lights say, 'Caution. Proceed carefully.'"

"But how do you give people a green light when you don't really know much about them?" Tom asked.

"Well, one way is simply to smile at them and be friendly. Another thing to do is listen and ask questions. Remember the power of initiating interest? And your nonverbal communication is really important during encounters with new people. When you have no history with a person, you must rely upon initial impressions, including body language. Think about it." Ron folded his arms and looked pensive to illustrate his point. "When you fold your arms, look around, or step away from a person, you are basically saying, 'I don't have any time for you.' Red light! But when you nod your head, make eye contact, and face the person you are meeting, he is much more likely to think you want to accept him."

"Okay, that's all logical. But what about ongoing relationships?" Tom inquired. "It seems like we Christians are constantly bombarded with the idea that we need to be taking moral positions, and upholding high standards. How can you honestly give a green light to someone who either proposes a lifestyle with which you disagree or makes a comment that contradicts your core beliefs?"

"That's a tough question," Ron responded, "but it's at the very heart of what makes the power of acceptance so strong. You see, most people naturally accept those who think and act the same way they do. I once read that the definition of admiration is 'the feeling you have when you meet someone just like you.'" Tom laughed. "So you see, we can easily give a green light to a person with whom we have a lot in common. But real ministry effectiveness comes into play when we are able to accept a person with unacceptable or disagreeable characteristics. Jesus did it constantly. He talked to the woman at the well, who was not married to the man she lived with, and he ate with the publicans and socialized with sinners.

"People don't enjoy being around those who reject them, who give them red lights. Unfortunately, Christians have often been the greatest violators of this very principle. They feel that it is their job to shower condemnation on a sinful world, to be divinely appointed finger-pointers. The way they do this is by rejecting everyone who fails to adopt a Christlike lifestyle, or who does not appear to comply with the code of ethics that the Bible promotes. Yet Jesus said that he did not come to condemn people but to save them."

"Ron, I hear what you're saying, but don't we have to take a stand? I mean, where do you draw the line between compromising on your standards and accepting people?" Tom asked.

"I don't think anyone with good sense would ever say that Jesus compromised on his personal standards, his holiness. On the other hand, some of the most religious people of his day accused Jesus of being a liberal socializer because they were major red-light hypocrites who didn't have a clue of who God really was. There is a very important point here—it is vital not to confuse acceptance of a person with approval of a behavior or an attitude.

"You see, Tom, when we confuse the two, we end up making principles more important than people. Jesus never compromised on his personal values, but he did not force them on other people. Likewise, he was constantly effective around those with deplorable personal lives, because he gave them the green light. He accepted them. And no one who knew him ever questioned his ethics. As a result, Jesus was able to make inroads into the hearts of some pretty seedy characters. He knew that people are mainly interested in one thing in life: love and acceptance."

"Wow, I need to think this one through," Tom admitted, "because that means I may need to soften up a bit in the way I come across to people I think are going down the wrong path."

Ron continued, "You see, when we communicate acceptance during times of conflict, we communicate unconditional love. When people tell dirty jokes, or let you know they think abortion is perfectly fine, or someone confesses to you that he is a homosexual, they are partially testing you to see whether you will accept or reject them. Once you reject them, you have more than likely jeopardized your ability to minister to them. The opportunity or ability to minister is an earned privilege, not a right. Of course, acceptance of a person may at first appear to be approval of a particular behavior or belief. Other Christians may even criticize you. That's a risk you take in cutting-edge ministry. But remember, Jesus' severest critics came from the religious community. And sometimes you have to pray for divine wisdom to know how far you can go in communicating acceptance before it becomes compromise. But, to be honest, Tom, I've found that much less of a struggle than trying to avoid a red-light attitude of rejection.

> ### It is not the nonbeliever's responsibility to establish a ministry relationship with a Christian.

"What I have found is that once people initially test you, and you pass the acceptance exam, they will then be open to hearing your views and will generally accept you as a person in spite of your differing views. It's like the old saying, 'People don't care how much you know until they know how much you care.' What happens with most believers who either intentionally or unintentionally end up rejecting others is that they blame their inability to minister on the nonbeliever's waywardness. But it is not the nonbeliever's responsibility to establish a ministry relationship with a Christian. That responsibility is ours."

"That all makes so much sense, Ron," Tom said thoughtfully. "It's such a good way to communicate love and acceptance and forgiveness. I suppose forgiveness is another green light we can give to our friends and family who offend us, for whatever reason."

"That's right. And remember, this ministry principle is also applicable between Christians. The weaker Christian, the one who tends to be either legalistic or too liberal in his attitudes, needs to be ministered to by a stronger brother or sister. The New Testament says we are to be accepting of both those who may not understand the lack of grace in legalism and those who are blind to the potential for sin and poor witnesses to the freedom available in Christ. Acceptance among Christians is the foundation for what the Bible refers to as unity in the faith. Ministry includes both outreach to non-Christians as well as support of our fellow believers."

"Ron, I'm tracking with you, but help me see how this fits into the concept of five-minute ministry. I know you pointed out that when you initially meet someone, your basic impressions are determined in the first five minutes of interaction, so you need to communicate acceptance. But why is the time issue so crucial in established relationships?" Tom inquired.

Ron sipped his water and stared at it while gathering his thoughts. "Generally, we communicate the acceptance or rejection of another person very soon after we interact on any level. When one of your subordinates blows it, and you have to confront him, your initial attitude will convey whether you are angry at him or at his behavior. When someone swears or gossips or tells a dirty joke that you find offensive, your first response will communicate your basic acceptance or rejection of the person. You don't have to laugh to show your acceptance, but the way you communicate your dislike for his *behavior* makes all the difference in how he perceives whether you value him. Like I said, people will often test you by sharing something that they think you will disagree with, just to see if your acceptance of them outweighs your nonapproval of their belief system. Your response may be as quick as a glance, a nod of the head, a smile, a frown, a turn of the body, or a brief comment. Remember, people are always more important than a set of rules. Any effective five-minute minister understands how important green lights are in establishing ministry ties. They occur throughout the day, and you don't have to go looking for them. Yet, without this understanding, you can unintentionally terminate potential ministry by rejecting a person who may be in need."

"Give the green light! I've got it," Tom affirmed.

Power Principle #4:

Ministry begins with acceptance, and we can communicate acceptance of another person during key opportunities of initial contact and potential disagreement.

For Reflection and Discussion

1. Think of a past or recent example of when you felt rejected by someone. How did it make you feel about future interactions with this person?

2. Discuss a real-life situation where you disagree with a person's behavior or idea, but still wish to communicate acceptance of that person. How do you handle the conflict?

3. Can you think of a time when you blew it with someone by failing to make the person more important than the principle?

4. Consider the "weak Christian"—or those who are legalistic and those who take advantage of their spiritual freedom. (Keeping the focus off things like drinking, abortion, dancing, smoking, etc., discuss the concepts of compromising too little or too much and how either approach affects our ability to minister.)

5. *Read John 8:1–11.* How did Jesus illustrate the power of acceptance?

5

The Power of Encouragement

---

*Encouragement expresses your faith by instilling
courage in others to hang on to positive expectations.*

Tom and Ron ordered lunch and were served. In
between bites, Tom jotted down further notes on the power
of acceptance. After passing on dessert, Tom asked, "What
is another principle for doing five-minute ministry?"

"Well," Ron continued, leaning
forward with his elbows on the
table, "the fifth power principle is represented by a
pompom."

"A what?" Tom asked, looking up from his notes.

"You know, the shredded paper or plastic mop ends that cheerleaders shake so enthusiastically," Ron smiled. "The image of a pompom best reflects the power of encouragement. This principle is similar to some of the other ideas you've learned so far, but it is so important that it really deserves its own category. Perhaps more than any single opportunity we have to communicate the concept of faith and hope in a difficult and painful world, encouragement is the answer," Ron explained.

"To be honest, I've never considered encouraging someone much of a ministry. I mean, it's a good thing to do, but how does it show Jesus to people?" Tom asked.

"We are most effective in showing Jesus when we address people at their point of vulnerability. The need for encouragement is a universal trait of humankind. Think how we frequently get beaten up during the course of a typical day. We fight traffic wherever we go. We get a call from the mechanic that fixing the car will cost more than was estimated. We face hassles at work, feel stress with our spouse, and handle conflict with our kids. The list goes on. Let's use a sports analogy. If a batter goes up to the plate and gets sideswiped by a wild pitch, he's more defensive, more cautious, the next time in the batter's box. And a tennis player who rushes the net, only to get a volley in the middle, is apt to stay on the baseline for the next play. The minor wounds we receive throughout the day tend to steal some of our courage. It's so easy to become discouraged. But a five-minute minister is a re-courager. That means being sort of a Johnny Appleseed when it comes to passing out words, notes, and comments that help people face their next challenge."

"I concur," nodded Tom, "but we both know that you can't always be encouraging, especially in the work world. People have to confront their failures and face circumstances that are not very encouraging."

"Sure, Tom, and it's important to realize that being an encourager means that you keep your feet firmly on solid ground. However, as a citizen of God's unshakable kingdom, we are not predisposed to base our responses on the six o'clock news, or the latest water-cooler rumor. Encouragement is not a denial of reality so much as it is a focus on the positive aspects of reality. Romans 8:28 says that 'in all things God works for the good of those who have been called according to his purpose.' If there is anyone who should be a purveyor of hope, it is the believer. It's a sad scenario when a Christian employee or citizen discourages someone and points out the negative possibilities.

"Tom, I know you're a positive person by nature, whereas many of us have to learn to be optimistic. But the job of the Christian is to be a remnant of hope in a decaying culture. Throughout the Old Testament, that is what God's people were expected to be, a bastion of faith and courage when everyone else was falling apart. One of my favorite illustrations about this is the buzzard that flew over a stretch of desert, found a carcass, and landed on it immediately. A hummingbird flew over the very same stretch of desert, spotted a flowering cactus, and headed for the blossom. The point is that we generally find what we are looking for. If you look for ugly decay, you'll find it, but you won't see the flower and its beauty. Our role as believers, as ministers, is to point out that God is sovereign and wise and good and wants the best for us."

"Naturally, my next question is, how do you do this without sounding preachy by saying, 'God is good. Trust in him— he's still in control'?" Tom asked.

"That kind of encouragement goes beyond the specific words you use. It's a matter of projecting optimism. Unfortunately, just because someone becomes a Christian, it does not mean he or she automatically becomes a positive person. But there is nothing as ironic as faith tinged with negativism. God never intended his people to be pessimists. We are salt, a preserving element, and light, a hope-giving quality. I know you've done some reading and study in the area of leadership," Ron commented.

"Sure," Tom acknowledged. "It's one of my favorite topics. What does that have to do with the ministry of encouragement?"

"Well, I have a theory," Ron suggested. "The reason why certain people emerge as leaders is that they are able to produce hope in others. Leaders are vendors of hope, and everyone is looking for that. All of us need hope to exist, to get out of bed, to make it through each day. People who have no hope turn to serial affairs, workaholism, materialism, drugs, and alcohol. Depression is total hopelessness. Discouragement is a lesser degree of hopelessness. HOPE means Hanging On to Positive Expectations. The primary mission of Jesus Christ was to provide hope for a lost and despairing world. Therefore, our objective as his followers is to be purveyors of hope."

"What does that have to do with leadership?" Tom asked.

"Oh, yes, I almost got sidetracked," Ron admitted. "Effective leaders attract followers because they are vendors of hope. Leaders have positive expectations and are able to influence others with their vision of the future. You cannot do ministry without that type of influence. When you express your faith by instilling hope in others, you become a minister of encouragement."

"That is interesting," Tom said in a thoughtful, drawn-out voice. "So what you're saying is that to be a minister means I must be constantly injecting words and ideas that spawn hope and positive expectations in those around me."

"That's pretty much it," Ron confirmed.

"Boy, I'm embarrassed to think of all the times I have responded with words or suggestions that may have burdened down Janet or my sons or my subordinates at work. Yet I'm not a negative person by nature," Tom confessed.

"Hey, no guilt here," Ron smiled. "All of us have done more than our share of *dis*-couraging. If we truly understood the power of our words, we would think twice about what comes out of our mouths."

"Well, just last week in our small group, we studied the passage in James where he talks about the power of the tongue. 'Who can tame it?' he asks," Tom recited.

Encouragement is expressing your faith by instilling courage in others to hang on to positive expectations.

"True," continued Ron. "When we gossip or complain or point out the negatives, we are reducing our ability to minister to a person or group. Words are manifestations of our faith. They reveal what is in our heart. When you open your mouth, is there love and encouragement, or hurt and gloom? 'Where seldom is heard a discouraging word' ought to be the slogan of all believers."

"So, again, how do I turn my office or home confrontations into ministry opportunities by being encouraging, yet direct and decisive?" Tom asked.

"Tom, it starts in your heart. That's the basis of all ministry. And I suppose I should mention again that true ministry is not so much a skill as an overflow of who we are. That's why God is so concerned with who we become on our Christian walk. He knows that regardless of how much we learn and what spiritual gifts we have, they are ineffective if not supported by godly character. Presuming that character development has taken place to a certain degree, we need to realize that the key to being confrontive and still encouraging is the target of our focus.

"What I mean is that an encourager is really a *re*-courager. He or she does not confront a person in the past tense, but instead suggests how that person might respond 'next time'—future tense. An encourager faces problems by seeking tomorrow's solutions, not rehashing yesterday's impossibilities. An encourager separates the behavior from the person and affirms the person's ability, past performance, and potential, while at the same time presenting the point of contention in a positive format. The important thing is the packaging, not so much the contents. Some Christians are under the impression that they cannot minister to people from a position of authority, but, confronting someone need not interrupt your ability to minister to that person. If it is done properly, it can communicate your caring. Even criticism can be expressed on an encouraging note, by presenting your belief in a person, not your disappointment. This whole concept of encouragement opens up our creative juices. You look for the best alternative instead of announcing to everyone that the ship is going down, so jump overboard. That might be an oversimplification. But does it help?"

"It does," Tom responded. "I see that it is up to me to apply it to my specific situations, but I never really considered how important my comments were in the context of doing ministry in everyday situations like work and home life. You know, we—or at least I—overlook how our attitude toward problems is a reflection of our faith in God and our world view."

"That's a great point," Ron congratulated. "As believers, our world view is that the end times will be ultimately good, not bad. We realize that our focus must not be on the present world, but on eternity. We also note that God can help us do greater things than we have done before. It is not so much that we tell everyone this as we go through the course of each day, but that such an attitude prevails throughout our responses."

"Right. So how do you encourage people specifically in five-minute segments?" Tom inquired.

"Well, there are basically two fields in which to use the power of encouragement in these brief ministry components. The first field is climate control, or situational encouragement. People are watching you all the time, just as you notice others. Every day, various situations arise that you respond to out of your position as a manager, a husband, a shopper, etcetera. The way you respond to a given situation creates an impression, a certain emotional climate. If your natural response is positive, hopeful, and basically optimistic, you communicate that uplifting force to others. People will also notice what you do *not* do. It's like the sun breaking through the clouds on a rainy day. For example, if you do not complain or gossip or tear people down, or suggest that there are no solutions available, they will take note. From your upbeat responses, people will form opinions about you that will make a positive impression, because hopeful people are not as common as the other sort. Then, if they discover that you have a personal faith in God, they will begin to put the two together, and their opinion of Christianity will automatically go up. The converse is also true. Christians who complain, exude a negative attitude, and purvey gloom and doom will turn nonbelievers off to God."

"I suppose the best thing a negative Christian could do is tell people he isn't a believer," Tom chuckled.

Ron laughed, too. "It is a bit of confusion of terms, isn't it? A negative Christian. What do they call that—an oxymoron?"

"So what is the other field of encouragement?" Tom inquired.

"Well, a situational response that produces a climate of encouragement is important. But the real playing field for

five-minute ministry is personal encouragement, which also
nearly always takes less than five minutes to complete. Again,
go back to the standard instruments of bridge building. Write
little notes of encouragement that say things like, 'Hi, just
thinking of you. Hope your day is going great. Have a super
week. Keep the faith. Don't give up. Keep up the good work.
I'm praying for you.' The world is full of discouraging words.
What we need to be in the church are encouragers. We
define the gospel as Good News. When we share it, we must
be good news, too. Make phone calls. Give hugs. Pat people
on the back."

   "How can you tell if people need encouragement?" Tom
asked.

   "Tom, I used to ask the very same question. I've never forgotten what the Five-Minute Minister told me. He said, 'Ron,
have you ever *not* appreciated an encouraging word?' That's
it! No matter how confident people appear, no matter how
much they get paid to do their job or how outgoing and bub-
bly they seem, they seek and need words of encouragement.
The world takes so much out of us that we do well to always
assume that everyone we meet will appreciate comments of
encouragement."

   "That's true," Tom remarked. "If someone says something
cheerful to me at the office or encourages me about a project I'm working on, I'll think about that for a long time afterwards. Our memories are sort of like echo chambers. I guess
it's like doing ministry, even after we're gone."

   "That's right," Ron affirmed. "And five-minute ministry
includes the consistent, simple, but powerful principle of
encouraging people. We are told in Scripture to encourage
one another in the faith. Never assume that another believer
does not need a good word. And when we encourage the
nonbeliever about the future, he will eventually see the cor-
relation between faith in God and hope for tomorrow. Everyone needs a cheerleader. Five-minute ministers shake the

pompom to build a positive spirit and courage and faith, because of the hope they have in a loving God who is in control."

"Rah! Rah!" Tom grinned, finishing up on his notes.

Power Principle #5:

Daily opportunities for ministry arise when we reveal the hope within us—by helping create a positive environment, by responding optimistically, and by re-couraging those with whom we interact.

For Reflection and Discussion

1. Without naming names, describe a person you know who is a dis-courager. Now, describe a person who is a re-courager.

2. Discuss the concept of how a person can encourage others and still maintain an objective approach to problem solving.

3. List some practical steps toward implementing the power principle of encouragement in your everyday world.

4. How do we undermine Christianity when we allow ourselves to complain, be negative, and allow discouragement?

5. *Read Philippians 4:4–13.* What are the various ways in which Paul encourages people in this passage? What situation was he in when he wrote these words? (*See Phil. 1:12–14.*)

6

The Power of Inside-Out Love

Most unloving behaviors are symptoms of low self-esteem and inner pain. People who base their worth on external affirmation focus on their own weaknesses and build emotional walls to prevent further injury.

When Ron looked at his watch, Tom did the same and asked, "Do we have time for one more ministry principle?"

"Let me call the office and let them know I'll be a little late," Ron answered, as he got up to find a pay phone. After he sat back down, he leaned forward with a smile. "Tom, let me give you one more power principle the Five-Minute Minister taught me. I think it is probably the most help-ful single idea I have ever learned in dealing with difficult people. The symbol of this principle is a stethoscope."

"A stethoscope," Tom muttered with a grin as he sketched an outline of one on his note pad. "This sounds intriguing."

"The stethoscope, of course, is an instrument that checks the physical condition of a heart. Using the power principle of inside-out love is one of the quickest ways to check the emotional heart of a person, in this case, his or her self-image. In less than five minutes, you can grasp some very vital personal information about people if you understand this fundamental law of human nature. Let me explain the concept to you, and then I'll show you how it pertains to five-minute ministry," Ron said.

"Fire away," Tom responded.

"The basis of inside-out love is the love passage in First Corinthians, chapter thirteen. You know, the one that starts with 'love is patient, love is kind,'" Ron explained.

"Sure, that's a great Scripture. We hear it a lot in Valentine's Day sermons and at weddings," Tom smiled.

"You've got it. However, if you understand the context of that passage, you'll see it is not simply talking about loving others. It is basically defining the term 'agape love.' *Agape* is the Greek word used to describe God's unconditional love for us. It is not an emotion as much as it is a choice, a decision of the will to treat another person as valuable. Although society's ideas of love include candlelight and violins, sex, and mushy sentimentalism, agape explains the way we should relate to others in our daily lives. What many people overlook is that it is also the word used in the verse that says we are to love our neighbors as we love ourselves. In essence, we are to use agape love on ourselves as well," Ron commented.

"Okay, we are to value ourselves and unconditionally love others. So where does this get us?" Tom pleaded.

"Well, let's put all of this into a practical format," Ron continued. "Let's say you're conducting a meeting, and one of the members is obnoxiously self-centered and aggressive. It is obvious that this individual is being counterproductive and creating group tension. As a group leader, you are inclined to either dismiss this person, confront him, or just follow your natural inclination to avoid contact with such disagreeable behavior. But how do you deal with this self-centered attitude and still hope to have any ministry to the person? The bigger question is, when people are unloving, and your first tendency is to avoid them, how do you maintain a caring mind-set?"

"That's a million-dollar question," Tom responded. "Unloving people are everywhere, and they are the last people on earth you feel like bothering with."

Ron nodded. "Ah, but the law of inside-out love states that when you see unloving behavior in people, it is a sign of what is going on inside them. You see, the scriptural definition of love is that it is patient, kind, not jealous, not envious, not easily angered, not boastful or proud or rude. It keeps no record of wrongs. It rejoices with truth and righteousness. Love always protects, trusts, hopes, and perseveres. Love never fails. Now, if we define agape love for ourselves as self-esteem, we know that when we do not have enough love for ourselves, we will not have love for others. You cannot give away what you do not possess. Therefore, when people do not show love for others, it is a sign that they do not have sufficient love for themselves. To sum up the principle of inside-out love, the person who demonstrates unloving behavior is not so much attacking others as he is revealing his own low self-esteem."

Tom seemed to chew on the concept for a while. Then he said, "So you mean that instead of taking a person's unloving attitude personally or seeing it as an attack, by applying the inside-out principle you are able to better understand what is going on inside a person. And if you understand that this unloving response is a symptom of low self-esteem, you are inclined to have empathy for him instead of being repulsed by him."

"You're a quick learner," Ron affirmed. "And true self-esteem is merely a psychological term for acknowledging God's love for you."

"Can you give me some illustrations of this?" Tom asked. "I mean, the concept makes a lot of sense, but I'm not sure if I would be able to know when I see it."

"Sure," Ron continued. "In fact, the love chapter in First Corinthians tells us what love is—and is not—by helping us identify thirteen common behaviors that reflect the degree of love within a person's heart.

Love inside out states that you can see most unloving behaviors in people as symptoms of low self-esteem and inner hurts.

"It's also a pretty good overview of most of the symptoms of low self-esteem. For example, love is patient. The person who exudes impatience is basically feeling that unless he obtains something at a certain speed, it is a mark against his self-worth. The man who just cannot wait for the waitress to seat him, or the woman who gets angry at her children's pace at a task, or the guy who blares his horn in traffic when the driver in front takes too long, are all projecting their lack of self-esteem. People who love themselves realize that their worth is not determined by how fast others respond to them or even how quickly they themselves are able to perform a certain task. When you see impatience in others, it helps you understand what is going on inside of them. When you sense it in yourself, it is a sign that you need to readjust your self-perceptions.

"Let me give you some more examples. The passage says that love is kind, which could best refer to considerate and friendly people. What do we look for in friends? We look for acceptance. Friends love us, warts and all. So, when a person is unkind and unaccepting by pointing out the things he doesn't like in people, he is revealing that he has not learned to accept himself, weaknesses and all. A very common way to detect this is by hearing someone say, 'Don't get me wrong. Gary is a really nice guy, *but* . . .' As soon as you hear the 'but,' you know you're not going to learn as much about Gary as you are about the person talking about him. You see, people with healthy self-esteem are able to accept the strengths and weaknesses in others because they have learned that their own value is based on being created in God's image, not on the world's standards of perfection."

"That's good," Tom said, not looking up from his rapid note-taking. "Give me some more."

"Well, let's look at another unloving behavior. The apostle Paul says that love is not jealous. At first glance, jealousy is perceived as hating another person because of what he or she represents, but jealousy is really hating yourself for not being like that person. It is playing the comparison game. As soon as you start basing your worth on how you measure up against others, you will always lose, because you will inevitably find people who are smarter, richer, younger, or better-looking, than you are. It's a dead-end road. At face value jealousy appears to be anger at others. It is really anger toward oneself. High-esteem people don't play the comparison game. They know we are all uniquely different yet equally valued by God. Envy is the same thing, only it is based on what others *have*. I think it tends to be more of a male weakness. We men have been conditioned to base our worth on what we own or achieve. When we see what someone else possesses or has achieved, we figure that our social worth would go up if we had the same, so we covet it and envy sets in."

"My goodness," Tom remarked, "I've really been blowing it with people like that. I never considered such an insight into their self-image. But what about people who are in love with themselves? You know, egomaniacs. How do you understand them?"

Impatience often reveals the idea that my worth is based on how quickly I achieve a task or how quickly others respond to my wishes.

A lack of acceptance of people or attributes often reveals that one has not learned to accept oneself, strengths and weaknesses. It is worth based on perfection.

Jealousy is hating yourself for not being like another person; worth by comparison.

Envy is being discontent with yourself based on comparing what one possesses or has achieved to others.

"The love passage tells us that love is not boastful or proud. The person who is full of pride and always bragging about himself is really *not* in love with himself," Ron said with a smile.

"Say what?" Tom puzzled. "Don't tell me that John You-Know-Who is not the most smug, self-satisfied guy you've ever met!"

"But Tom," Ron cautioned, "when you realize that John's boastfulness is really only a pseudo self-love, you'd realize that it is a facade. You see, self-esteem, our evaluation of ourselves as worthy individuals made in God's image, is vital to emotional and spiritual health and maturity. When we lose that perception, we often try to fake it. Pride is play-acting, a poor imitation of the real thing. A braggart is constantly trying to win the approval of others. He is trying to get everyone to think what a great guy he is. Only if they approve of him can he approve of himself. He is depending on others for his sense of self-worth. But high-esteem people realize that their worth is not based on what others think, so they do not need the false security that pridefulness seeks to provide. They do not depend on others' applause or affirmation.

"The inverse of exaggerated pride is rudeness. A woman who does not value herself may try to put others down by pointing out their weaknesses and faults. Or a man with a poor self-image may make little snide remarks or comments to or about another person, drawing unnecessary attention to the mistakes in a report or a poor job performance. However, because high-esteem people realize there are no perfect humans or perfect performances, they do not need to point out everyone's shortcomings or behave in other discourteous ways. Rude people are also playing the comparison game, but instead of trying to lift themselves above everyone else like braggarts do, they try to lower everyone else in the eyes of the world by making certain weaknesses evident. A person who is rude is basically revealing his or her own insecurity and feeling the need to hurt another. Demolishing someone else's reputation does not make yours look any better.

"In that same trilogy of false self-love is what the Bible calls 'self-seeking.' Egocentrics demand that all their needs be satisfied by others. Selfishness is rampant in a culture that teaches us to expect instant gratification. Some self-centered people, for example, want only to talk about themselves. They think that listening means simply waiting for their turn to jump into the conversation. But that kind of a person has lost something very valuable: a sense of self-worth. When you misplace a prized possession, all your emotional energies go into finding it. Our self-esteem is our most prized possession. People who have lost theirs strive to replace it, and some of them do so by calling attention to themselves. They may exhibit this by being a class clown, trying to get the biggest laugh. Others reflect their insecurity by acting shy and retiring to avoid being embarrassed, certain that everyone is looking at them. Extreme self-consciousness is debilitating, and it's irritating to those around us." Ron paused, waiting for Tom to respond.

"So you're telling me," Tom summarized, "that when we see people who are boastful, or rude, or self-centered, they are really hurting individuals, and these offensive behaviors are merely unhealthy attempts to regain their self-esteem?" Ron nodded agreement.

"Wow! That could really help me deal with such individuals. I used to be offended by people like this, but now I'm seeing that they are really wounded victims."

"You're right, Tom, and that's where ministry comes into play. When you see these people as hurting, instead of abrasive and annoying, you will be able to approach them at their real point of need and ignore their irritating ways. Plus, it keeps you from taking their unloving response personally," Ron added. "And it also helps you recognize when your self-esteem is low."

"So true," Tom responded. "Can you give me a compact version of some other unloving behaviors?"

"Sure," Ron continued. "There's a great book on inside-out love I can give you, but here's an overview. When the Bible says 'Love is not easily angered,' it is telling us to realize that people who are irritable and quick to react with hostility feel threatened. Anger is usually a defensive response. Love and self-esteem make us feel comfortable and safe. A lack of this security causes us to perceive people and circumstances as enemies. An animal fights back when it feels threatened, and insecure people tend to lash out at every problem and people in general as dangerous situations. This person is typically hard to deal with unless you apply the law of inside-out love. Then you quickly deduce that his anger is a response to his inner hurt, his feeling of being threatened. If you see the insecurity behind the anger, you are less likely to be intimidated and turned off by hostile people.

Pride and boasting tend to be pseudo-self-esteem and are attempts to lift oneself up above others, depending on others for affirmation and self-worth.

Rudeness, putting others down, is an attempt to make others appear lower than oneself in comparison.

Self-centeredness reflects a person's aim at gaining attention, in hopes of creating self-worth, which has been misplaced.

"Now, another unloving behavior is lack of forgiveness. People who keep records of wrongs—who hold grudges, seek revenge, or at least refuse to let go of past hurts—have not learned to forgive themselves. Mental hospitals are full of such people, and it's a major cause of neuroses. For example, a woman with low self-esteem believes she cannot be forgiven for her flaws and projects that feeling onto others. She cannot forgive people for times she has felt they offended her. You see it constantly when people are bitter about ex-spouses. Or grown-ups still complain about how they were treated by their parents. People pour out their poison about a past friend, former pastor, or ex-employer—anyone who has let them down. There are a lot of wounded people walking around who have not learned that the primary benefit of forgiveness is self-healing. God wants us to forgive, not only to show our love for others but to heal ourselves when we feel wounded. The person who cannot muster forgiveness when offended is basically holding on to the pain by rehearsing the offense over and over and over again. Why would anyone voluntarily replay a personal insult? Because in that person's heart is the feeling that he or she somehow deserved the insult. Again, high-esteem people realize that their value is not determined by how others treat them. They learn that the best thing they can do for themselves is to forgive the hurt so that it does not fester and ruin their attitude toward life itself. So, when you see someone who is bitter and harbors a grudge, it is a sign that this person is suffering from low self-esteem.

"Next, love rejoices in truth and righteousness. People with a sense of self-worth want what is best for themselves. In essence, they seek excellence. Holiness is moral excellence. People who do not value themselves tend to treat their souls and bodies recklessly. They are self-destructive. The most obvious form is suicide, wherein you devalue your life so much that you actually end it out of disgust. We usually throw away what we perceive as worthless. But less obvious self-destructive behavior includes drug abuse, promiscuity, and alcoholism. Even symptoms like obesity, the fear of success, and questionable moral and ethical behaviors tend to reflect a low self-view. When people who value their lives also discover that God and his righteousness are the most excellent way, they pursue it, not out of a legalistic, have-to attitude, but out of love and affection for others and themselves. Those who do not value their lives tend toward a worldly, less wholesome lifestyle. When you understand this as a minister, you no longer find yourself abhorring those who do not seek God with your enthusiasm. Instead, you desire to love them and help them seek what is best for them."

"I'm tracking now," Tom replied. "I know you're pressed for time, but can you just give me the gist of the remaining inside-out behaviors and then tie it into the idea of five-minute ministry?"

"No problem," Ron chuckled. "Let me tell you about the final components of this law. First, love always protects. Love makes us strong on the inside. To love others we must allow ourselves to be vulnerable, so we risk being hurt. Being a loving person does not mean you can avoid being hurt. It does mean realizing that your self-worth is not based on others' acceptance or rejection of yourself. Here's a great illustration. A crab is a sea animal that wears a hard, external shell to protect its soft, squishy insides. Crabby people, the ones who are hard and cold and crusty on the outside, really are just soft and hurting on the inside. Our normal reaction to these people is rejection: 'Yuck, I don't like being around them.' But when you apply the law of inside-out love, you realize that their prickly behavior is really a defense mechanism that protects them from further hurt. The problem is that not only do their emotional walls keep out potential harm, they keep out love as well. And the crabbier they are, the more you know they are trying to protect their soft, squishy insides. If you treat them lovingly, you strengthen their resources by building up their self-esteem."

"Next, 'love always trusts' refers to the idea that people of high self-esteem believe in the goodwill of others. People who have few friends and never get beyond a superficial level of communication have usually been hurt in the past and therefore are unwilling to trust again. Such people also tend to be low achievers, because to accomplish anything you have to set a goal, and that means taking a risk. If they take that risk and fail, they might be ridiculed, and because they base their worth on what others say and what they themselves achieve, it seems a risk too big to take. The worst side effect of low self-esteem is not being willing to trust God. We are not born with the ability to trust. It is nonexistent until we have a reason to do so. That is why the Bible tells us about God's great love for us before it asks us to trust him. Love must come before trust. If you meet people unwilling to trust, it is a sign they are hurting and suffering from low self-esteem."

Easily angered people are responding defensively, as they perceive others and circumstances are threatening their security.

Those with little interest in truth, who indulge in self-destructive behaviors, and who live a lifestyle which does not enhance one's value as moral excellence does, are reflecting a low self-worth. (Why wash, wax, and put expensive tires on a clunker?)

A lack of forgiveness is a sign that one bases self-worth on others' responses, and even embraces the hurt by replaying the insult in one's mind.

"The next phrase, 'love always hopes,' is related to the power principle of encouragement. People who have a healthy self-image tend to be positive and optimistic. People who focus on what is wrong with their lives tend to be negative, gloomy, and see only the problems they face. It is helpful to realize that when you interact with negative persons, their sense of self-worth is probably reflected as cynicism. You see, people who are noticing the negatives in their own lives tend to see the negatives in others and in every situation. High-esteem people concentrate on the positives in life and in others because they are looking at that in their own lives and have hopeful expectations.

"Finally, 'love always perseveres' refers to the ability to keep on loving someone when he or she does not return our love. Most people really don't give love; they trade it. You can see this everywhere in business. If you scratch my back, I'll scratch yours. You be nice to me, and I'll be nice to you. But really, the only proof of whether what you have is agape, God's love, is if it is unconditional—no strings attached. True self-esteem is not something that comes from the outside; it exists within you because God has put it there. If you depend on external love to determine your self-worth, you will forever be sporadic in your ability to love others. God loves us from the inside out. We can love the unloving if our sense of value is based on God's love for us, not on others' acceptance or treatment of us."

"Man, I think I'm going to have to go over these notes with you in a few days. Thanks, Ron. I have one last question," Tom asked. "How does this fit into a five-minute ministry framework?"

"Well, it fits basically in two ways," Ron explained. "First is prevention. When you see one or more of these unloving behaviors in another person, by quickly applying the law of inside-out love, you can avoid responding poorly to this individual. You see, if you respond according to your first impulse, you will tend to alienate or offend the other person. It is very hard to minister to a person against whom we have put up barriers. So what this concept does is allow us to understand where a person is coming from and prevent us from making a wrong diagnosis. That's where the stethoscope image comes in. You're actually listening to the person's heart, not just making a wild guess about his emotional and spiritual health. Diagnose the behavior as a self-revelation rather than as a personal attack.

Aloof, cool, crabby behavior reflects one who has been hurt in the past, and has built up emotional walls to prevent further injury.

An unwillingness to take risks in goal setting and being vulnerable in relationships reflects a belief that one's worth comes from achievement and acceptance of others.

A negative, critical attitude tends to express one's internal focus on what is not right in oneself.

An inability to love when others stop loving is a sign that self-worth is based on external affirmation by others versus internal affirmation by God.

"The second way this pertains to five-minute ministry is in prescribing the antidote. When you apply this principle, you can very quickly, without much fanfare or extensive counseling, begin to administer the solution to the real problem—low self-esteem. Begin building this person up as an individual with real worth, instead of treating him as an irritating person who has a lot of hang-ups. It is important to address the real versus the felt needs. When you get to the root of human problems instead of just treating the symptoms, you are well on your way to winning people for Christ, or at least ministering to them with Christ's love. Jesus tells us to pray for those who persecute us. The only way we can do this effectively is to see them as victims, not enemies. Again, this can be done in typical interactions that transpire throughout the course of a day."

"I see it now, Ron. The stethoscope represents a quick analysis of the heart and helps me respond to the real needs. But now we have to run. Thanks again," Tom said as he glanced quickly at his watch. The two men rose and shook hands. "I am so thankful that you and Maryann are willing to help us learn these principles. It's making a big difference in our lives," Tom added at the door.

After dinner that night, Tom sat down to review the notes he had taken during his lunch with Ron. Taking out his Bible, he read 1 Corinthians 13 and realized that what his friend had told him about inside-out love as a principle of ministry put the apostle Paul's words in a practical light. Tom took out a legal pad and drew up the following list of what love is—and is not. Then he added some ideas that he might be able to use in five-minute ministry.

> *Love is patient.* When I am impatient or irritable, I am revealing that my sense of self-worth is dependent upon how quickly I can achieve a given task or how readily other people respond to my wishes and do things *my* way.
> *Love is kind.* Unfriendliness to those around me or intolerance of their shortcomings is a sign that I have not completely accepted myself, both my strengths and my weaknesses. True self-esteem is not based on perfectionism.
> *Love does not envy.* Jealousy implies that I really hate myself for not being like some other person. It bases my sense of worth on comparisons. Envy is similar in that it, too,

shows I am discontented with the way I am because others have more possessions or have accomplished more than I have.

Love does not boast, it is not proud. Bragging and excessive pride tend to be pseudo self-love. They are attempts to lift oneself up in the eyes of other people and to gain their approval and admiration. Boasters are play-acting.

Love is not rude. People who use put-downs and other forms of discourtesy are trying to bolster their own sense of worth by making others seem inferior.

Love is not self-seeking. An egotist acts as if the world revolves around his existence. Because he is basically lacking in self-esteem, he either constantly demands the attention of others or hides his insecurities in shyness to avoid being embarrassed.

Love is not easily angered. Hostile people may have been hurt in the past, so they respond defensively to any individuals or circumstances that they perceive as threatening to their own security.

Love keeps no record of wrongs. If we are unable to forgive, we are really saying that our self-esteem is tied to how others have treated us. By holding grudges, we embrace the pain by replaying the insults over and over again.

Love does not delight in evil but rejoices with the truth. If we value ourselves as God's creatures, we will respond to his holy truths by seeking moral excellence and by avoiding self-destructive behavior.

Love always protects. Aloof, cool, and crabby people are protecting themselves from harm by building up an emotional blockade. By loving them, we add our strength to their own resources and help them recognize their value as a lovable individual.

Love always trusts. An unwillingness to take risks in goal setting and relationships reflects a belief that our worth depends on externals—measurable achievements and the approval of other people.

Love always hopes. A negative, gloomy attitude tends to express an internal focus on what is not right with one-

self. Because optimistic people are acknowledging the
positives in themselves and others, they can face difficult
situations with hopeful expectations.
Love always perseveres. An inability to love someone who does
not return love reflects a view that relationships are a trad-
ing game. When we are able to love the unloving, we
affirm that God's love for us is unconditional and can
internalize the strength that comes from this knowledge.
Love never fails!

Power Principle #6:

*Numerous opportunities for ministry
arise when we observe or are confronted
by the unloving responses of others.
Inside-out love involves diagnosing these
symptoms as a disease and prescribing
the antidote: unconditional love.*

For Reflection and Discussion

1. Which of the ideas about inside-out love did you find the most insightful?

2. Think of two people you know who exhibit some of these unloving traits consistently. What have you learned about them from this chapter? How will you respond differently to them now that you've learned the power principle of inside-out love?

3. What unloving behaviors do you tend to resort to when your self-esteem level is low? How can these serve as signs that you need to rethink your self-perceptions?

4. How would you use a five-minute approach to minister to the people mentioned in question #2?

5. *Read 1 Corinthians 13:4–8.* What other life examples could you give to illustrate what love is and is not, as listed in this passage?

7

The Power of Sensitive Moments

The inner core of a person is nearest the surface during times of change that result in either extreme joy or severe pain.

"Good morning, Janet," Maryann said, giving her friend a big hug. "It's good to see you. Come on in."

"How are you?" Janet asked. "I hope your frantic schedule is giving you some breathing room."

"Ron and I learned years ago that you always make room for things you really want to do, so life is really just a product of one's priorities," Maryann explained. "And today is Saturday, and I've got time for conversation and coffee!"

The two women walked into the kitchen and sat down at the round table near a bay window glowing with sunlight. Maryann poured coffee for her guest as she asked, "Janet, how have things been going in your part of the world?"

"Oh, Maryann, things have never been better. I mean, the kids are doing great in school and work is fine, but this five-minute ministry stuff has really added a new dimension to our lives. Tom and I have grown closer together while learning and discussing those power principles. He has ministered to me and the children several times by focusing on opportunities to accept us in tough times and encourage us during stressful moments. I had once thought of ministry as something that you do for other people, but it's also something you do for your own family."

"That's true," Maryann responded. "Maybe down the road we can talk more about parenting and marriage and how five-minute ministry works in those areas. But ministry is being Jesus to whomever we meet."

"After he met Ron for lunch, Tom came home and explained three new concepts: the green light, the pompom, and the stethoscope," Janet continued. "That stethoscope principle, the law of inside-out love, is really incredible. I'm sure I've only grasped part of it, but it has revolutionized the way I see unloving people and react to them. Believe it or not, I actually got to the point of inviting this lady at work to church, but a month ago she was driving me up a wall."

Maryann laughed. "Tell me more."

"Well, this gal was one of those negative, cynical, grouchy people who looks twenty years older than she is. Everyone just sort of avoided her, or put up with her at best. When I got to thinking about the idea of inside-out love and that love always protects and always hopes, I realized that Joan wasn't really a mean, sour person intentionally. She probably had some major hurts in her life. So I made friends with her. It turns out that her husband died not long ago, and her grown kids live across the country. She felt alone and in pain. Maryann, you ought to see Joan now!" Janet exclaimed. "I have people come by my desk and make comments like I must be a saint, to talk to grouchy Joan, but even they agree that she's much more pleasant these days. I think she's coming to our Bible study group this week. We'll see."

"Janet, that is so great!" Maryann congratulated. "That principle alone has done so much in our ministry and saved us many frustrations with others. I'm very glad you and Tom are learning to apply the Five-Minute Minister's ideas. Sometimes when people hear them, they consider them too simple, too easy, so they end up never even trying them out. That means losing out on more and more ministry opportunities."

"Well, I don't want to make us sound like experts," Janet explained. "I'm sure we miss opportunities all the time, and sometimes when we see them we get nervous or rushed and don't respond to them, but at least we're *seeing* them. And we are getting some good results, like with Joan."

"Ron and I are proud of you two," Maryann added.

"So, what's next?" Janet inquired. "What are some more of the ten main power principles of five-minute ministry?"

"You don't waste any time, do you?" Maryann laughed. "Okay, ready for notes? The next principle is represented by a rose."

"Is this sexist?" Janet chuckled. "Tom never mentioned one about a flower."

Maryann chuckled as well. "No, the rose in this case represents the power of seizing tender moments, whether they are joyful or sad. A rose is delicate, gentle, soft. It is the symbol of a person's emotions when he or she experiences a crisis or trauma or even a happy event. Remember what you learned about the windows of opportunity that open up in a person's life?"

"Sure," Janet affirmed.

"Well, there are many windows of receptivity to ministry in a person's life, and quite a few are related to significant rites of passage. They are special enough to deserve their own ministry principle. Major life-changing events may be a divorce, new birth, the loss of a job, moving, a parenting crisis, facing mid-life, marriage, or health issues. Responding sensitively in these crucial times, will both show you care and enable future ministry to take place."

"I understand the point, but why does it take a minor or major crisis situation to make people sensitive to ministry?" Janet probed.

"I think it probably goes back to a common human dilemma," Maryann explained. "The very first sin had to do with the temptation to challenge God's sovereignty. The essence of all sin is basically making yourself your own god, or at least putting yourself before God. Many cults promise to show you how to become a god. For example, the New Age movement talks about the goodness and power within you. I think it's that all of us, in varying degrees, like to make ourselves into little gods. We think we can control our lives and call the shots. But, during times of change, and especially negative ones like the loss of something significant— a loved one, a spouse, a job, money, or our health—we all of a sudden are drastically reminded that our little god has let us down and that we are not as in control as we often believe ourselves to be. We are most open to establish contact with the true God when we realize we have unsatisfied needs in our lives."

"So you're saying that I can effectively minister to someone during times of hurt and a feeling of powerlessness," Janet echoed.

"That's pretty much it," Maryann responded.

"But, in the case of negative situations, I mean where people lose a job or discover they have cancer or have a parent die, I don't know what to say. More than once I've put my foot in my mouth and said something silly, and now I find myself pulling away because I'm not sure how to respond," Janet confessed.

"I know what you mean," Maryann nodded. "We've all gone through similar situations. But you see, the five-minute idea of ministry is great here, because it means that effective ministry need not be lengthy or even poetic. The key is sensitivity to others' delicate emotions. You could drop off a card, or make a brief phone call, or even just give someone a hug and say, 'I believe in you. If I can help in any way, I'm here for you.' The problem is, we often let important ministry opportunities go by. We either ignore them or are fearful of appearing awkward or unsure. In fact, one reason why loving a person during an emotional time can be so effective is that most people avoid those in painful or negative situations. If you reach out instead of looking away, you'll make a positive impression. Some people give negative support, but you will stand out if you provide something positive."

"What do you mean by negative support?" Janet asked.

"Negative support occurs when a person is trying to convey comfort and affirmation but goes about it in a negative way, so that the end result is less than uplifting. For example, when a woman is going through a marriage separation, some friends will gather around and say, 'Hey, just get rid of the guy. You're too good for him.' That doesn't necessarily help her make the best decision. Or, when you were pregnant, did you ever have friends or complete strangers, come up and tell you some horror story about a cousin who spent a whole day in heavy labor?"

Janet laughed. "You, too?"

"Even if people mean well, they can do more harm than good," Maryann explained. "So, if you provide a sample of positive, sensitive support, you will often be as welcome as a cool drink in a desert."

"I relate to that," Janet responded. "It helps a lot knowing I don't need to have all the answers, or some magic wand to make things better."

"True, you don't need a secret formula to do good ministry," Maryann agreed. "The Holy Spirit is all the 'magic' you need. What he needs is people who will make that point of contact so that ministry can take place." Maryann poured

Janet more coffee, then asked, "Janet, have you ever gone whale watching off the coast?"

"Well, we haven't gone out on a boat just to watch whales, but we have seen them migrating from the shore. It's magnificent," Janet replied.

"It is," Maryann nodded. "Every year, like you said, the whales migrate, and only during certain seasons are they visible. They are swimming under water most of their lives, but for brief moments, we catch glimpses of these majestic mammals."

"Am I losing something here, or did we switch subjects?" Janet smiled.

"Both," Maryann smiled in return. "We know that people are emotional beings. They have joys and fears and dreams and problems all the time. But, during certain times, their inner lives are near the surface, touchable, observable. These are the sensitive moments when ministry can create long-term benefits."

Janet had been sipping her coffee in between jotting down notes and responding to her friend's explanations. Now she sat still a moment, staring at her cup while she thought about this concept. "What about the good times?" she asked. "I see why negative crises would make people open to the idea that they are not in charge of their lives and that perhaps they do need a higher power than themselves, but why would positive events also serve as sensitive times?"

"Well, I think it's probably another sort of migration," Maryann responded. "I've found that one of the best ways to get to the root of someone's core self is to ask subtle questions about his or her dreams or significant life events or relationships. Events like marriage, giving birth, and a significant promotion provide open windows through which you can see into a person's inner life. Our emotions tend to be closer to the surface during these times. Those are our tender moments. As a child, did you ever become a blood sister with a friend?"

"You mean where you make an oath of commitment to each other and prick your fingers and mix blood?" Janet asked.

"That's sort of it," Maryann agreed.

"No, I know what you are talking about, but I never went through that ritual."

"I never have either," Maryann admitted, "but it sort of explains the special bonding that takes place between people when at least one of them is experiencing a significant high or low in life. Times of intense joy and pain often make us vulnerable. Symbolically, our lives get pricked by these events or episodes, and when others lovingly touch us, a special bonding takes place that cannot be replicated. It may be quick, but it is often deeper than relationships established before and after such an episode."

The inner core of a person is nearest the surface during times of change resulting in extreme joy and extreme pain.

"I can think of an example of that," Janet suggested. "When I was in labor with Robbie, our first child, two of our friends rushed over eighty miles to be with Tom and me during that time. Terri and Leonard let us know they were there, and Terri actually helped out in the delivery room when things looked a little tense for a while. Then she went home, but she came back to stay with us for a few days when the baby and I left the hospital." Janet paused to reflect on the memory. "Yes, she will always have a warm place in my heart for her ministry to me during that happy but scary time as a new mother."

"That's a good example," Maryann affirmed. "Obviously, that involved more than five-minute ministry, but the principle is there. As you learned at our first meeting, effective ministry can often take place in short, key situations that at times open themselves up for more prolonged, intensive ministry opportunities. I've learned from the Five-Minute Minister to take special notice when I meet someone who is going through a significant up or down time. I always try to respond sensitively to such people. The Bible says to weep with those who weep and rejoice with those who rejoice. Jesus performed his first miracle while celebrating at a friend's wedding. One of the shortest but most significant Bible verses refers to Jesus' response to Mary and Martha at the loss of their brother, Lazarus: 'Jesus wept.' And when Jesus was hanging on the cross, he looked at the pain and aloneness of his mother and told John to take care of her. You see, ministry is looking beyond your own concerns, and addressing the needs and emotions of others."

"This is really helpful," Janet commented as she wrote more notes. "The rose signifies the power principle of seizing tender moments. I suppose if we fail to seize these moments, they will close up and be lost to us."

"Like a fresh rose, they will wilt and often be gone forever," Maryann agreed. "Sometimes, we lose our ability to minister if we wait too long to do anything, even though the condition continues."

"What do you mean by that?" Janet inquired.

"I mean that when a person is going through a certain high or low time, and she knows we are aware of it, but we do not respond to the opportunity, we have lost the immediate effect of being sensitive, and the other person may perceive our subsequent concern as insincere or superficial," Maryann explained.

"Whew! That means we really do need to make the most of those brief, often spontaneous situations," Janet sighed.

"God wants us to be sensitive to ministry cues around us," Maryann continued. "That's the beauty of five-minute ministry. It is based on the idea that most ministry opportunities come your way naturally. You don't have to deviate from the way God leads you on a daily basis. You just have to remain alert and sensitive to those key situations when they surface."

"So let me run this by you," Janet said, looking at her notes. "When I meet or hear about people experiencing important life events, whether they be loss of a job, divorce, parenting problems, mid-life, childbirth, marriage, moving, financial difficulties, or poor health, I need to realize that these are windows of ministry opportunity. Five-minute ministry involves recognizing them and making appropriate responses to the situation, because during those tender times people are most open to ministry contact."

"Right on," Maryann affirmed. "Most of these events reflect times of passage. Change pries us from our routine comforts and stability and control and causes us to be aware of our limited powers. Good or bad, sensitive moments tend to be stressors, so we respond more positively to ministry contact. You've got it!"

Power Principle #7:

Key times for ministry take place when we respond sensitively to those going through positive and negative crises surrounding life events.

For Reflection and Discussion

1. List some tender moments in your life history, both good and bad.

2. Can you think of a stressful time of change in your life when you were open to ministry from others and did or did not receive it?

3. Who around you now could benefit from such sensitivity? What could you do?

4. Discuss with your spouse or a friend some possible responses to someone who might be sensitive to ministry at this time.

5. *Read John 11:33–36 and 19:25–27.* What do these passages tell us about the power of sensitive moments?

8

The Power of Support

You can learn a lot about a person by listening to what he or she says or does not say about someone who is not present.

"Would you like any more coffee?" Maryann asked, holding up the pot before she poured herself a cup.

"No, thanks," Janet responded, "Two cups is my limit."

"It's decaf," Maryann said with a smile.

"I'm fine, really. Besides, I'm ready for the next five-minute ministry principle."

"You're relentless, and I love it," Maryann chuckled. "Well, quite frankly, this power principle sounds simplistic, but it really goes a long way, not only in spontaneous ministry, but in what it does to provide for future ministry opportunities. It is called the power of support, and it is represented by a walking cane. A cane is what you lean on, so it gives you support."

"What kind of support are we talking about?" Janet inquired.

"We are talking about the emotional security you give to others when you avoid gossip or slander and, instead, are verbally supportive of people," Maryann explained. Janet wrote down some notes and drew a picture of a cane. "Are you ready for more?" Maryann asked.

Janet looked up with a smile, "Fire when ready."

"Janet, are you ever with other people, maybe there are only one or two of them, and the topic of discussion moves to a person not present in the group?"

Janet laughed. "Is there ever a time when that doesn't happen, especially in women's conversations?"

"All right, you get the setting," Maryann continued. "To misquote the Bible: 'Where two or three are gathered, there is someone discussed in their midst.' Anyway, it's very common social behavior to talk about someone who is not present. An opportunity for ministry arises when the comments about another person are either unloving or uncomplimentary, and this prompts you to share something that is supportive of that person."

"So you mean the walking-cane idea has to do with supporting the person being talked about?" Janet asked further.

"Right," Maryann confirmed.

"I guess I don't see how that is much of a ministry," Janet commented.

"Let me explain it further," Maryann suggested. "James says, 'With the tongue we praise our Lord and Father, and with it we curse men, who have been made in God's likeness. Out of the same mouth come praise and cursing. My brothers, this should not be' [James 3:9–10]. Five-minute ministry comes when we recognize the opportunity to say something good about another person. We either jump in with our verbal support of that absent person, or we silently communicate our unwillingness to participate in talking about someone who is not there. All of this is very brief, but it goes a long way."

"I think I see your point," Janet sighed, "but who are we ministering to—the person being talked about or the people in the group?"

"Good question," Maryann affirmed. "Both. Whenever you provide support for people who are not present, you do two things. First of all, you minister to the absent person, because we all know that gossip, comments, and grapevine experiences usually get back in part to the subject of the conversation. Therefore, when the person being talked about hears that you affirmed her in her absence, she will feel a great respect and appreciation for you, which will in turn open up doors for future and greater ministry. Second, and what is often overlooked, is that you can minister to those in the group, whether it is a single person or several, by supporting the person who is absent."

"How does this work?" Janet asked.

"You minister to them with your integrity by not participating in uncomplimentary discussions of someone who is not there to defend herself. In doing so, you communicate emotional security to the others. What I mean is, when you affirm another person in front of others, or at least avoid saying anything negative or derogatory about her, you tend to build a bond of trust and minister safety to the others. Therefore, even people who say less than favorable things about others will turn to you for support later. When they find themselves needing counsel, they will more than likely seek you out."

Janet wrote more notes. "This is great, Maryann. Oh, I don't know how many times I have failed on this one. It is so easy to get caught up in petty conversations about others."

"Janet," Maryann said, leaning forward, "just between you and me, on the whole I think women are naturally more sen-

sitive to emotional needs than men are. When you read the
Bible, you see how, time after time, women were responsive
to the needs of others around them. Women washed Jesus'
feet, stood with him at his crucifixion, and were the first to
discover his resurrection. Because we tend to be more relational, we talk more about people in everyday conversations,
whereas men often talk about less interpersonal things, like
business, sports, finances, or whatever. But Janet, I think
that women also tend to be more guilty of failing to support
others in conversations. I have let myself get caught up so
many times in the destructive practice of talking about other
people behind their backs in unkind ways. And it usually
happens so innocently, so matter-of-factly."

"But Maryann, you are the most affirming woman I have
ever met," Janet responded. "I can't imagine you saying anything less than constructive about another person."

"You haven't heard me talk about *you!*" Maryann teased.
"Just kidding. I love you." The women laughed. Maryann
leaned back in her chair and continued. "Let me give you a
few Scriptures that have to do with this ministry principle."
She pulled out a piece of paper with her handwriting on it
and read: "Titus 3:10 says, 'Warn a divisive person once, and
then warn him a second time. After that, have nothing to do
with him. You may be sure that such a man is warped and
sinful.' We usually think of the terms 'warped' and 'sinful'
as referring to wicked people like serial killers, perverts, and
adulterers. You know, *real* sinners. But here they refer to an
attitude: a person who spreads words that are divisive.

"I think the best basis for this power principle is Ephesians 4:29–31, 'Do not let any unwholesome talk come out
of your mouths, but only what is helpful for building others
up according to their needs, that it may benefit those who
listen. And do not grieve the Holy Spirit of God. . . . Get rid
of all bitterness, rage and anger, brawling and slander, along
with every form of malice.' The key meaning of that passage

is that we are to share according to a person's needs and say only what will benefit those who happen to hear our words. Most complaining and derogatory comments are not to help another person. They tend to come from our own improper motivations."

"What about last Sunday's message?" Janet added. "You know, the verses that say we'll have to give account on the day of judgment for every careless word spoken. For by our words we'll be acquitted, and by our words we'll be condemned."

"Convicting, isn't it?" Maryann responded. "That's Matthew 12:36–37, I have it here on my list."

"That is a scary thought," Janet commented. "I never considered careless words a big deal. Blatant hatred, screaming, yelling, taking God's name in vain—those were big deals. But careless words just sneak out. You want to be a part of a conversation, so when the discussion turns to people, you just sort of add your two cents' worth, even if it's uncomplimentary."

"So true, and the Five-Minute Minister says that in those select times we have three options. The first option is to do what comes naturally and share the negativity, endorsing in your own words what others are saying. The second option is to comment on what you *like* about the other person or what he or she is good at. The third option is to say nothing. Sometimes silence speaks louder than words."

"How does saying nothing provide support?" Janet asked.

"Silence says you willfully choose not to get involved in gossip or speculation or negative commentary. By doing this, you minister by modeling to others that if one can't say something good about a person, it is better to say nothing at all. You also let people know loud and clear that you are safe to be around. When people share with you negative things about others, you consciously or subconsciously realize that they will most likely also talk about you when you're not around. Even though friends do this, it tends to build up walls of defense and separation. When you consistently support others by focusing on their good aspects and avoiding criticism and other negative remarks, you become somewhat of a refuge where people can turn if they need to talk."

"I guess that's what Jesus did when the men brought him the woman caught in adultery," Janet added.

"I think so," Maryann agreed. "I have watched the Five-Minute Minister do this several times over the last few years. A while ago, when a nationally known religious leader had a moral failure and everyone was talking about it, some of us were discussing it during our Bible study. A woman in the group noticed that the Five-Minute Minister was not sharing his views, so she asked him, 'What do you think?' He quietly said, 'You know, all of us are just one step away from such a fall.' Wow, talk about convicting! I'll never forget not only the change of course in the remaining conversation, but also the certainty we all felt inside that he was right."

> ### *You learn a lot about a person by what she says or does not say about others.*

"But doesn't that seem sort of holier-than-thou?" Janet rebutted. "I don't mean that in disrespect, but the real world sort of expects you to give your opinion."

"Janet, that *was* a 'real world' incident," Maryann explained. "But I think I know what you mean. Whenever you choose to be a change agent, a minister, you run the high risk of being misunderstood. The misunderstanding about Jesus' ministry led to his crucifixion. We seem different when we minister, because most people do not minister. Therefore, ministry stands out. Christians should not let the world squeeze them into its mold. I think what you are getting at refers to the attitude in which ministry is done. If you have a high-brow, finger-pointing approach and reprimand people for talking about others, you may be just as guilty as they are. Jesus was pretty harsh with the Pharisees, who acted so spiritual and religious yet condemned people who were not exactly like them. The power of this ministry principle is more in what it doesn't do than in what it does, because the most natural thing to do when others are talking about someone is to chime in and participate."

"Okay, I get the idea," Janet confirmed. "But what about an honest discussion about someone who has a problem, or a work situation where the person is failing? You sometimes have to deal with relational issues that are not always positive."

"Good question," Maryann complimented. "I think the key there is given in the Ephesians verses we talked about. Only share 'what is helpful for building others up according to their needs, that it may benefit those who listen.' The Five-Minute Minister taught us a helpful term: *worthless reality*. Although something may be true about a person—for example, he may be angry, or she may be irresponsible—if it does no good to mention it, it is worthless information. Just because something is real doesn't give us the right or the need to bring it up.

"So, if there are people listening who are not part of fixing the problem, it is best to stay supportive, or at least silent, until you can discuss the person with those directly involved with the situation. Otherwise, the listeners will not benefit from hearing your comments, and they will not perceive your words as ministry. Now, once those who are directly affected by a person's problem are together, the focus of your comments needs to be on that person's needs. Usually this is done by separating the offensive behavior from the person as much as possible. Character assassination is unloving and counterproductive, whereas behavior modification is usually an achievable goal."

"Can you give me an example of this?" Janet asked.

"Sure, last week at work, one of our vice-presidents sent out a somewhat harsh memo about the secretarial pool tak-

ing advantage of their lunch hour and breaks. As office manager, I was aware of both sides of the issue, but you can imagine the havoc such a memo would create! Although I felt
frustrated by the way the message was transmitted and listened to the staff talk about it, I supported the vice-president
by affirming her concern for team building and asking that
a few not ruin it for the rest of us. You see, anything I would
have said to criticize the VP would not have been sensitive
to her motives in sending the memo, and it would have also
communicated a lack of loyalty on my part. Loyalty is an
important ministry character trait. Unless you convey trust-
worthiness, it is hard to have effective ministry. When others see you as loyal to someone else, they feel you will be loyal
to them as well."

"So how did it turn out?" Janet pursued.

"Well, as I said, I provided a listening ear, but I avoided con-
firming the staff's negative comments about the vice-president.
Sometimes, we get mixed up in believing that having a sym-
pathetic ear requires agreeing with another person's critical
comments. You can communicate concern without joining in
the rock throwing. Anyway," Maryann continued, "after the
water-cooler conversations, I called the VP for a meeting. Then
I confronted her with my thoughts about the memo. And, in
revealing the concerns of the staff, I supported them by not
putting them down by saying things like, 'You know how sec-
retaries are,' or 'There's been some gossip going around the
front office about you recently.'"

"That's sure a good example of using this principle," Janet
affirmed.

"A big part of five-minute ministry is recognizing those
brief opportunities and making the most of them," Maryann
explained. "James was right when he talked about the power
of the tongue. Our goal is to put out conversational fires.
When you put in unhelpful comments, it's like throwing
another log on the blaze."

"In other words, you should either pour water on the fire or just let it die out on its own," Janet added. "But is this really ministry? I think my old concept of ministry keeps coming back to haunt me."

"Your idea of ministry is probably still expanding," Maryann confirmed. "Five-minute ministry doesn't give you time to go to seminary or resort to theological commentaries or even don a robe and other priestly attire. But everyday life is the sort of stuff that most ministry opportunities are made of. The way you minister by providing support is that you show others what Jesus would do. He did not participate in the condemnation of others, and he was constantly supporting people by his words and affirmations. The power of support sees opportunities to stick in a prop where a person's character may be sagging, or under fire, whether or not she is there to defend herself. In doing this, you not only model a Christ-like attitude of love, but you communicate to all the people present that they can be safe with you. They will then feel you would in turn support them during similar conversations when they were absent. When you participate in insulting commentary or even just share truthful tidbits that fail to edify a person in her absence, you are kicking out her support—taking away her cane."

"This is good stuff," Janet responded. "I'm glad you taught me this one. I'll get a lot of mileage out of it."

Power Principle #8:

Frequent ministry opportunities arise when people talk about someone in less than favorable terms. By affirming that person's positive qualities, or at least remaining silent, you model support and communicate emotional safety to others.

For Reflection and Discussion

1. What is a recent example of a conversation you heard that did not benefit the person being discussed? (No need to share specific names.)

2. How could you have applied the power principle of support to that situation?

3. Can you think of a time when you saw this principle modeled, or when you learned that someone supported you in your absence?

4. Discuss some ways to provide emotional support without appearing judgmental to others or overly spiritual.

5. *Read Ephesians 4:29; Matthew 12:36–37; and James 3:9–10.* What do these passages tell us about this ministry concept?

9

The Power of Integrity

People are looking for those who are authentic and who have integrity. They are watching to see if you are one such person.

Birds chirped outside Maryann's kitchen window while the two friends sat discussing five-minute ministry. The morning sunlight came streaming in at such an angle that the beams appeared to be celestial affirmations of their conversation. This was a happy time, Janet thought, a chance to learn life-changing principles of ministry that she could

actually practice in her everyday life. Ministry, she was discovering, was not so much a time commitment as it was a timeliness commitment. She knew in her heart that using these power principles really can make a difference in others' lives. It is a way of being Jesus to people who may or may not know him already.

"How are you doing?" Maryann inquired, interrupting Janet's reflections. "Are you game for one more five-minute principle?"

"I'm ready," Janet responded. "I was just appreciating this morning and our friendship and the wisdom behind those principles. I'm amazed at how simple they seem. And they are everyday occurrences."

"Everyday *opportunities*," Maryann critiqued. "Ministry rarely happens accidentally. It is almost always a result of being tuned in to fertile situations and responding intentionally to them."

"If we keep going, we'll need to add a 'reverend' to our names," Janet joked.

"That's not too far from the truth. With all due respect for our pastor and other trained professionals, I believe that God wants us to be priests in our homes, neighborhoods, offices, and other circles of influence. When you start thinking of yourself as a priest, it changes your self-image and how you respond to certain situations. In fact, that is a good introduction to the next ministry principle: the power of integrity," Maryann explained. "The power of integrity is represented by a nugget of gold. The concept is that ministry opportunities arise in everyday living whenever we make choices that reflect our character. By the decision we make at these pivotal points, we either model Christianity, or we lose our spiritual influence upon others."

"This sounds a little bit like our last principle, the power of support through the spoken word," Janet reviewed. "That had to do with verbal integrity."

"You're right, Janet," Maryann affirmed. "But the power of integrity is broader than just verbal support. Because it involves the will and our actions, it is more of a character revelation than words alone. The word *integrity* comes from the word *integer*, which means one, or whole. When we lack integrity, we lack wholeness. Remember those verses from James that we studied a few weeks ago in Bible study, the ones that referred to people who were double-minded?"

"Right. Double-minded people should not expect to see their prayers answered, because God hates double-mindedness," Janet commented.

"Those are the verses," Maryann responded. "Basically, being double-minded means we lack integrity or wholeness that we are not what we claim to be. It is very hard to minister when we are divided in our character. In fact, some people will actually test you to analyze your integrity."

"What do you mean?" Janet asked. "You mean they set traps for you?"

"It often is not malicious or quite so premeditated, but all of us humans want to know what other people are made of," Maryann explained. "We want to know who we are dealing with, and if they are really as we perceived them at first glance."

"I'm sure there are countless examples, but please give me a couple, to be sure I know what you are talking about," Janet requested.

"Sure. Let's see," Maryann said, pausing to think about an appropriate example. "A couple of weeks ago, Ron shared with me a ministry opportunity that arose at work. He and a leading salesman of the company were entertaining a representative of a potentially good customer. The client seemed to be very interested in a contract with the company, but the salesman hinted at the possibility of providing some special benefits, which would have involved fixing the bid and 'thanking' the representative with personal payoffs. It was not obvious or down in black and white, but everyone understood what was going on. Although he was very gracious, Ron recognized a key ministry opportunity, so he verbalized the company's adherence to excellence and trust and high integrity. He told me that the climate changed very quickly."

"So what happened?" Janet asked. "Did the other two men fall on their knees and ask God for forgiveness?" Both women laughed. "I'm sorry, Maryann, you know I was just kidding. I thought you were setting me up."

"Of course, you know that sort of dramatic reaction is only a minor part of ministry, but it almost only happens as a result of making the most of previous five-minute ministry opportunities," Maryann explained. "Anyway, they didn't sign the deal that night. The salesman was obviously provoked by Ron's interference and told Ron that this was how things worked in the real world. Ron stood his ground and said that if they couldn't get deals without compromising their integrity, they shouldn't be in business. Well, two days later, the salesman just happened to drop by Ron's office, and he apologized about the scene he had made after the meeting. Then they got to talking about personal things, and Ron had a chance to give him a recent tape from church on marriage."

"Don't tell me," Janet teased. "The potential client called back and doubled the original order."

"No," Maryann chuckled. "It's all still pending. But the point is that great ministry can take place in such brief situations, crossroads where we have to choose either the golden way or the way of compromise. It is hard to have effective ministry after we have compromised our standards. Jesus' followers got to see his integrity constantly, when he was up or down, by himself or with the masses. All of us have been influenced by others as we've watched them handle a moral or ethical dilemma."

"I guess you and Ron have ministered to Tom and myself in this way. I never stopped to think about it," Janet admitted. "We've commented from time to time about your love for each other, and how you deal with each other when you're having an apparent disagreement or point of contention. It has set a good example for us and also made us value the other things you have shared with us."

"That's so nice of you to say," Maryann said, looking down at her coffee mug. "I think if there is anything that injures our Christian witness and, in essence, our ability to minister effectively, it is in not taking seriously enough the power behind integrity. James tells us to be doers of God's Word and not hearers only. That means not being a hypocrite, a word that refers to actors in ancient Greece, who would often wear a mask when they played the part of a character in a play. Ministry opportunities arise when we are called to reveal whether or not we are wearing a mask. It may be a comment about a social issue, the response to an ethical question, or a decision we make to tell a white lie rather than the truth.

People are looking for those who are authentic and who have integrity. They are watching to see if you are one of them.

"I once heard the pastor tell about the ancient pottery merchants who displayed their wares at the market. Some potters would take slightly cracked or damaged pots, fill the defects with wax, and pass them off as first quality. A customer could tell the first-quality from the wax-filled pots by holding them up to the sun or a bright light. Honest merchants would put a sign by their wares that read 'sincere,' which literally means, 'without wax.' Ministry opportunities arise when people hold us up to the light and see that we are sincere, that we don't have cracks in our character."

"But, Maryann, that's too much pressure," Janet moaned. "How can anyone keep that sort of high-quality lifestyle, day in and day out?"

"I guess there are two possible responses to that," Maryann explained. "The first response is that you're right—no one can. We will likely fail from time to time, as John said in his first epistle, because no one is without sin. And it is unfair for people to judge Christianity by its followers who are unable to live out all its dynamics. The other response is that we can't respond with integrity every time unless it really is a part of who we are. You see, pressure doesn't build character as much as it reveals it. Before I reveal the fruit of the Spirit, the Spirit needs to be working within me, in changing my very core. The point of five-minute ministry is not so much 'faking it till we make it,' as it is recognizing that our ministry will be greatly promoted, or greatly reduced, by how we respond in key situations."

"So I hear you saying that when we don't respond with integrity, like when we pick the less ethical solution, we have hampered our ability to minister and in turn have missed out on a ministry opportunity," Janet reviewed.

"Right." Maryann pulled another piece of paper out of her Bible and read: "Philippians 1:27 says to always let your conduct be worthy of the gospel of Jesus Christ. Proverbs 10:9 says, 'The man of integrity walks securely.' Integrity is in short supply, so when you demonstrate it, even though you don't do it perfectly, you will make an impact on others. They will notice it.

"There come times when people want to know if our faith and our character have cracks. No one is faultless. Most people don't expect perfection. But they do want authenticity, wholeness—integrity."

"It seems to me that a lot of what you have been talking about is not only applicable on the job and with our neighbors, but it also fits well in the home," Janet commented.

"Our most important ministry *is* in our homes," Maryann affirmed. "It says in First Timothy that our home life is fundamental to leadership in other ministry areas. And it is in the home that opportunities to model integrity make the greatest impact, specifically with children. You've probably heard the passages in Scriptures that say a father should not 'embitter' or 'exasperate' his child. I think the thing that creates the greatest frustration in a child is seeing double standards in a parent. When the parent says one thing and does another, the child watches, and feelings of tension and discouragement intensify, often silently. As Christian parents and workers, we sometimes think we can get away with compromise, because often no one says anything, but the Five-Minute Minister told us that people do take note, whether or not they say anything about it."

"So you're saying that when I tell my son to go clean his room, he looks at our messy garage," Janet said with a sheepish grin.

"Bingo!" Maryann cheered.

"Whew! This ministry stuff holds you accountable, doesn't it?" Janet sighed.

"It does, but the best thing is that it helps you become the person God really wants you to be," Maryann responded. "You see, as long as I'm aloof to my ministry opportunities, and as long as I do not consider myself a priest to my family, neighborhood, or co-workers, I can pretty much do as I please. We all know that those who do as they please usually do not develop the discipline that growth and reaching your potential require. To be honest, I think we laypeople have subtly liked the idea of ministry being the responsibility of the professional clergy, because it removes the pressure from us to live as Jesus would live."

"Talk about conviction, that's a bit heavy for a Saturday morning," Janet said with a nod. "I suppose I'm as guilty of that as anyone, without even thinking about it. But what about those times when you do blow it? You know, when you turn your back on an indiscretion, or change the figures on a bid, or compromise on the truth, or relax a standard of some sort? Are you saying that the chance to do ministry is lost? No one is perfect."

"I hope I've not given the impression that we have to be morally perfect to have a ministry," Maryann apologized. "It's true that we lose certain opportunities for ministry when we are silent or when we go along with the compromises of others. But the beauty of being a Christian is that repentance is an option. Repentance is not only an issue between you and God, it is also a matter of acknowledging wrong choices and trying to correct them so others will notice. Sometimes, the very fact that you walk up to a person and apologize for not taking a stand, or you turn around and share your remorse, can make a great ministry impact. You see, admitting you are wrong is often more difficult than making the right decision in the first place. When you share your convictions afterwards and demonstrate a sensitive conscience, you can often regain that ministry of integrity."

"That's comforting to know," Janet responded. "I am thinking right now about a situation in which I need to do just that thing. I've got to talk to a person at work and let her know I was wrong in letting something happen that was in an ethically gray area. But how do you avoid being seen as a goodie-two-shoes, you know, a moral zealot? It seems like that might alienate people so that you couldn't minister to them."

"You always run that risk," Maryann agreed, "just as we discussed in supporting others. However, more times than not, we lose more in making poor decisions and not taking advantage of ministry opportunities than we do in taking appropriate stands. Most people want to do what is right, and they often want someone else to show them the way. The majority silently search for credible, authentic people. When they see integrity in you, they will not only be personally encouraged, but they will more than likely look to you for future interaction."

"When I think of people in my own life, I find that to be very true." Janet reminisced. "I do remember instances when a person made an impact on me by how he or she responded to certain situations. They were not always major decisions either."

"Again, the key is that we recognize what those opportunities look like and then respond quickly to them," Maryann affirmed. "Here's a quote I love from Charles Spurgeon: 'A good character is the best tombstone. Those who loved you, and were helped by you, will remember you when forget-me-nots are withered. Carve your name on hearts, and not on marble.'"

Janet looked at the clock on the wall. "I can't believe where the time has gone. This has been so helpful. Can you give me a summary of this concept again before I need to go? I know we've talked about several different issues related to the power of integrity."

"Sure, Janet. Just remember what Job said: 'When he has tested me, I will come forth as gold.' That is the essence of this principle. The gold nugget symbolizes the positive influence we can be if we take advantage of brief opportunities that arise during the course of our daily lives. If others see that our behavior consistently duplicates our words, they will be far more willing to respond to our ministry than if our character fails that test. Whenever we seem to be double-minded, our integrity is in question, and we are decreasing our ability to influence them in the future."

Power Principle #9:

Significant ministry can take place when we respond briefly and effectively to specific opportunities that call on us to reveal our character by reacting with integrity.

For Reflection and Discussion

1. Describe a situation where a person you had respected failed the integrity test.

2. Describe an integrity challenge you presently face, explaining how you can make it into a ministry opportunity. (Or draw on a recent experience to illustrate this principle.)

3. Discuss some of the finer issues of being a Christian in a non-Christian setting. Explain how you can take an ethical stand without alienating those around you.

4. List some biblical characters who either compromised or stood firm during integrity challenges and describe what resulted from their actions.

5. *Read James 1:22; 2:14–26.* What do these passages have to say about the power of integrity as a principle of ministry?

10

The Power of Humility

Humility is communicated by:
    1. Saying, "I'm sorry. I was wrong," or "Thank you," or "What do you think?"
    2. Absorbing rather than rejecting blame
    3. Humor in general and toward oneself
    4. Sharing weaknesses
    5. Active listening

"Well, did you enjoy our fellowship group tonight?" the Five-Minute Minister asked Tom and Janet as they sat down in his family room after the others had left.

"It was as wonderful as ever," Janet responded. "These are really neat people."

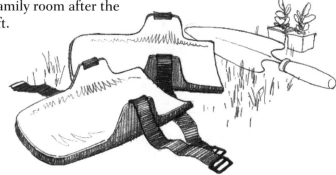

"They are," their host agreed. "One of the practical problems with these meetings is that everyone stays so late because they enjoy each other's company! But I'm glad you were able to stay to wind up our five-minute-ministry power principles."

"We look forward to this fellowship group every week," Tom added. "It's sort of an oasis from the work world and other pressures. But I must admit, work and home life and our extracurricular activities in general have been more and more exciting as we have come to recognize and take advantage of ministry opportunities, thanks to the new concepts we've learned. Janet and I really appreciate how you, Ron, and Maryann have introduced us to these ideas!"

"Yes, and thanks for inviting us to stay after the regular meeting," Janet added.

"Well, if everyone had the enthusiasm and teachable spirits that you two have, this world would be a different sort of place," the Five-Minute Minister affirmed.

"That's nice of you to say," Janet smiled, "but I don't see how any person who has even a moderate love for Christ and concern for spiritual growth could fail to implement and get excited about this concept. I mean, we're no Billy Graham or Mother Teresa, but Tom and I now recognize the biblical truth that we can do ministry."

"Yes, and we don't have to go out and create ministry opportunities," Tom inserted. "They come to us disguised as ordinary problems, decisions, and interactions with people."

"I like what I'm hearing from you two," the Five-Minute Minister said. "Before I tell you something about having a ministry mind-set in general, I wanted to describe one more power principle. Is it fair to assume that Ron and Maryann gave you the last several items?"

"We met with them one-on-one for some of the concepts and then shared with each other," Tom responded.

"The three that Maryann taught me had to do with sensitive moments, support, and integrity," Janet explained. "The last one made me think pretty hard about some recent interactions at work. In fact, I ended up going back to one of my supervisors and apologizing for not taking a stronger stand for some ethical principles that contradicted certain recent decisions."

"I like the way you worded that," the Five-Minute Minister affirmed. "Integrity is not so much being *against* the wrong things as it is an issue of standing *for* the right things. That perspective helps you have a more positive attitude about bucking the tide."

"When Janet told me about the principle of support, it caused me to think more about my everyday conversations," Tom confessed. "One of our neighbors is—how shall I say it?—challenging to have in our association. From time to time, when other neighbors drop by, they usually get around to complaining about this man. Since learning the principle of support, I've tried to be more a listening ear than a co-complainer. I'm not sure what effect it has had so far, but I sure feel a lot better after these conversations, and I've even put in a good word for the guy."

"Good," the Five-Minute Minister said, with a loving, relaxed demeanor. Then he leaned forward in his chair, as if to say something important. "Tom, Janet, you are doing what Jesus hopes for all believers: to hear the word, and obey it. The secular must become sacred, meaning that we need to perceive our work, home, and personal life as viable places for God to work. Likewise, the sacred must become secular. In other words, the ideas we glean in worship and Bible study need to be implemented in our daily lives. There is a danger in separating our spiritual life from other facets of our life. D. L. Moody said, 'The Scriptures were not given to increase our knowledge, but to change our lives.' You are becoming change agents because you are *changed* agents.

"The last power principle is not necessarily more or less important than the rest, but I think it really helps make all other ministry attempts more effective and palatable. It is possible to turn people off when we buck normal human or sinful responses in life, but is very difficult to reject a person who is humble. So the tenth power principle is humility, and it is aptly represented by the symbol of a knee pad. Obviously, the knee pad conveys the idea of kneeling or bowing down before someone. When one of these ministry moments backfires, it is often due to a lack of perceived humility in the minister."

"I understand what you are saying as far as humility being important, but how do you minister through humility?" Tom asked.

"Humility becomes a ministry both directly and indirectly," the Five-Minute Minister explained. "As I mentioned, it can indirectly minister by making our ministry actions seem genuine and earnest. Because we all have unique personalities, we respond differently to various ministry opportunities. God made us that way, so we need not think effective ministry comes only from certain temperaments. However, regardless of our personality traits, we tend to create emotional barriers when those we are trying to influence perceive us as lacking humility."

"Humility is not exactly a popular subject these days," Janet commented. "I've yet to see a best-selling book with that word in its title."

The trio chuckled together. Tom continued, "That's true. And 'Win by Intimidation,' or 'Looking Out for Number One,' are hardly Jesus-sounding titles."

"Exactly," the Five-Minute Minister chimed in. "That is the reason why humility can become a direct ministry influence."

"I don't get it," Tom admitted.

"I'll explain," the Five-Minute Minister said, leaning back in his chair and staring at the ceiling as if to glance at a mental note card. "Let me give it to you this way." He held up his hand, fingers extended. "There are five significant ways to minister through humility. Each is a response to a potent situation. The first has to do with three golden phrases. They are, 'I'm sorry. I was wrong,' 'Thank you,' and 'What do you think?'" He paused to allow Tom and Janet to write in their notes. "By saying, 'I'm sorry. I was wrong,' during important times of confrontation or revelation or personal interaction, you are admitting to being imperfect. Now everyone knows that no one is perfect, but by admitting it in a specific situation, you take away the other person's desire to *prove* you are imperfect. Those words are very effective when they come from someone who is doing ministry. The next phrase, 'Thank you,' means that you are grateful for being the recipient of another's service. It says, 'I acknowledge your work and your life.' It is out of our neediness that we receive service from others. Thereby, 'Thank you' strongly communicates the idea of ministry. Max DePree said, 'The first responsibility of a leader is to define reality. The last is to say thank you. In between the two, the leader must become a servant and a debtor.'"

"But that is so contrary to what happens in the corporate world," Tom countered.

"All the more reason why it makes an impact," the Five-Minute Minister responded. "Did you ever wonder why a jeweler shows off his diamonds by placing them on a black velvet cloth?"

"So they stand out," Janet answered.

"Exactly," the Five-Minute Minister said. "Philippians 2:15 says we are to be 'blameless and pure' so that we can shine like stars in a darkened generation. Stars seem brightest when the sky is the darkest. Because the world's culture is not thankful and tends to encourage pride in self-sufficiency, we make a greater splash when we are thankful and acknowledge our needs. The final phrase, 'What do you think?' means you know you don't have all the answers. You want to consider another person's opinion. Whether you are a CEO or a parent, one of the most effective ways to gain someone's trust and communicate humility is to seek out another's opinion."

"That is true. And it's so simple," Tom declared.

"The second way to minister through humility," said the Five-Minute Minister, pointing to his index finger, "is absorbing blame. When something goes wrong—a letter did not get mailed, an engagement is missed, a phone call never gets returned—you take the wind out of a person's sails when you absorb their blaming words."

"But what if you were not responsible?" Janet asked. "I know people who are trained to say 'I'm sorry' as a manipulative tactic, whether they are wrong or not."

"I know what you mean," the Five-Minute Minister responded. "By absorbing blame I do not mean admitting blame if you are innocent. Absorbing blame is like a foam cushion's response to someone's jumping onto it from a tall height. It softens the fall and then bounces back gently. When you reject or toss back the blame, like a basketball against a backboard, you communicate pride and insensitivity. By letting other people vent their anger, and then responding empathetically and softly to them, you are communicating humility.

"A third way to respond humbly involves humor. Humble people are able to laugh about themselves and about life in general."

"What if you're not a comedian by nature?" Janet asked.

"You don't need to be," the Five-Minute Minister said with a smile. "But lightheartedness or the ability to laugh with others really tears down emotional barriers. Jesus used humor several times in his teachings, even though most of us do not recognize it because humor tends to be culture-oriented. When you are able to laugh at key times, especially at yourself, you let others know that you do not take your-self too seriously, and therefore you are easy to be around. Some people have the idea that Christians are always seri-ous party-poopers. A good healthy laugh, even if only when sharing a clean joke or cartoon, raises the spirits of those with whom we interact."

"I never considered humor a ministry," Tom admitted. "It's nice to think that representing Christ can involve laughter."

"So true. A fourth humility response involves sharing weaknesses," the Five-Minute Minister continued. "Obvi-ously, this is where wisdom comes into play. For example, shared weaknesses can work against you when you are in a competitive environment. However, there are select times when sharing a fear, a story of failure, a character flaw, or some other imperfection can effectively draw the other per-son or persons into your life. We tend to compare our insides with others' outsides, and in so doing feel threatened by them. But if we can judiciously admit a weak point, we min-ister through humility."

Tom interrupted with a comment: "It seems like there comes a time in your life when you get so tired of proving yourself strong and perfect that you really admire those who are confident enough to admit their weakness. But don't you think men have a harder time with this than women?"

"I think they do," the Five-Minute Minister agreed. "As more and more women take on corporate roles, they might lose this beautiful spirit, but as a rule, I think men feel a greater need to keep up the appearance of strength and courage that goes with a machismo image. That's why a man who is humble can often make a great positive impact. Let me give you one final humility response. It's called listen-ing. Good old-fashioned, attentive listening."

"I may be able to guess, but why is that a sign of humil-ity?" Janet asked.

"Take a guess," the Five-Minute Minister suggested.

"Well, I suppose it's a sign of humility because when you really listen, you are not claiming to have all the answers, like you do when you are talking or waiting to interrupt," Janet answered, taking her cue to continue. "I think that when we listen, we stand out in the crowd because so few people do it. Most people are mainly interested in telling you *their* story and *their* problems and *their* solutions. Talking can become a pretty prideful thing to do."

"I'd say that was an excellent guess," the Five-Minute Minister responded. "Effective listeners are involved in the speaker's words but avoid advice giving, blaming, and trivializing his or her concerns. In so doing, you endear yourself to others and bolster their self-esteem by your display of meekness."

"But honestly, does meekness really work in the real world, especially in the corporate jungle?" Tom interjected. "I'm not sure that just because something is different, it can be ministry. Wearing an orange wig might be different, but it sure isn't ministry. And it wouldn't be good for business either."

The Five-Minute Minister laughed, unruffled by Tom's counterpoint. "Everything in life has parameters, limitations. The parables, for example, were intended as earthly stories with a heavenly message. Some people take them out of context by trying to make every character or action mean something in and of itself. I don't mean to suggest that just because something is out-of-the ordinary, it is ministry. However, when we are ministering, we are representing Christ and reflecting his lifestyle, and we will sometimes stand out. Meekness is definitely a Christ-like trait, but it is not a position of weakness. Meekness is quiet strength. Most people like to wear their résumés on their lapels, so everyone can read them and know how great they are. Like Little Jack Horner, who stuck in his thumb and pulled out a plum and said, 'What a good boy am I,' they want everyone else to recognize their admirable qualities. But the second chapter of Philippians says our attitude is to be the same as that of Jesus, 'who being in very nature God, did not consider equality with God something to be grasped.' Rather, he took the form of a servant and submitted himself to death on a cross. That's the attitude of brokenness, humility, and meekness that God wants us to have. No one can deny the power of Jesus as revealed in the Gospels, but knowing who he was—the Son of God— he was able to remain meek. It is out of our human insecurities that we refrain from humility and strive to prove ourselves. Meekness allows our true strength to emerge on its own, without fanfare or exaltations. Jesus, who was rich beyond measure, became poor, so that out of his poverty, we may become rich and enrich the lives of others. Our poverty as humans is expressed in our humility. Jesus demonstrated this best when he washed his disciples' feet. Ministry opportunities arise daily when we can either wash other people's feet, so to speak, or we can refuse to wash their feet, implying that we expect them to wash *our* feet. It probably took less than five minutes per person to wash each disciple's feet, but it made a lifetime impact on them, as it should on us. For example, think about a person you admire, someone you look up to either now or as a young person."

"I think of a professor I had in college," Tom shared. "She tended to be sort of quiet, but she saw something in me that encouraged me."

"Was she an unpretentious woman?" the Five-Minute Minister asked.

"Very much so," Tom admitted.

"The person I was thinking of is modest, too," Janet expressed. "He's sometimes very outgoing, but there is an underlying sense of strength, peacefulness, and caring. You just enjoy being around him and want to emulate his attitude toward life."

"Yes," the Five-Minute Minister agreed. "I suppose that our models have varying degrees of humility and show it in different ways, but a humble spirit is what empowers all servanthood, and therefore all ministry. Humility acknowledges the insufficiency that we share with our fellow humans and then expresses our gratitude for God's provision through helping others in their need."

Power Principle #10:

The display of a humble attitude at key times provides direct and indirect ministry to others.

For Reflection and Discussion

1. Describe someone you know who does not show humility. How does that make you or others feel?

2. Think of a situation where you could minister through humility.

3. Describe the qualities of a person you admire, or someone who had an influence upon you as a young person. Was humility one of those qualities? How was it revealed?

4. *Read Philippians 2:5–11 and John 13:1–17.* How did Jesus exhibit humility in these passages?

Epilogue

God created our lives to evolve around concentrated moments of ministry that we can accomplish while we do our ongoing tasks.

The Five-Minute Minister sat back with a smile, "Well, Janet and Tom, there you have it—the ten power principles of ministry you can do as you go about your daily routine. Pretty simple, aren't they?"

"You know, when we first began these lessons, I thought we were going to learn something way out, you know, ideas I'd never even heard of before," Tom shared. "I *have* learned plenty of new things, but it's sort of old things in a new context! This has revolutionized the way I perceive ministry and my role as a Christian in general. I underestimated the impact that such simple, focused practices can provide."

"Right," added Janet. "I guess for me, I feel as though my whole concept of Christianity has been turned inside out. I've just never taken it seriously that I, a layperson, could really implement ministry in my everyday interactions with people. All this makes so much sense and helps me understand other aspects of Scripture and my Christian faith. I want to know if there are principles like these for other parts of my life."

"Yes, Janet, there are some ministry principles that apply to specific relationships like parenting, and marriage, and leadership. They, too, are all somewhat simple. But simple doesn't always mean easy," the Five-Minute Minister replied. "What Jesus meant when he said, 'My yoke is easy and my burden is light,' is that life itself is hard and burdensome, but Christianity is not meant to be. Although God knows there is no way most people can commit all their energies to serving him by ministering to others, he never puts us on the shelf and considers us hopeless. Christians have been intimidated in the past by the idea of being used by God and doing ministry. Yet how depressing is the thought that my primary purpose in life was to go to college, get a job, work my way up, make money, retire, and die! I have to believe that just as some men and women are called into full-time Christian service, my vocation is to minister to everyone whom God brings across my path. Solomon said that when he surveyed all that his hands had done and what he had toiled to achieve, everything seemed meaningless, a chasing after the wind: 'There is nothing new under the sun.' True happiness means understanding the difference between making a living and making a life. I realize that my work place, my social circles, and my neighborhood are merely communities in which I'm called to do ministry, to meet people's needs by revealing Jesus. Peter says we are to 'live such good lives among the pagans that, though they accuse you of doing wrong, they may see your good deeds and glorify God on the day he visits us.'

"That's why I think that God, when he created life as we know it, planned to put a majority of our ministry opportunities into concentrated, key situations. Therefore, while we're working or shopping or going to school or relaxing at the beach, we are expected to respond to those opportunities that come our way. That's what five-minute ministry is all about. I remember as a young boy, going into our garden to pick tomatoes. I would yank at the green ones and leave some of the juicy, vine-ripened ones untouched. Most ministry opportunities do not need to be created or yanked off the vine. They are all around us. We just need to learn to recognize them and pick the ripe ones. Those in turn open up more opportunities for deeper and more involved ministry times, in which God may or may not choose to use us."

"What happens when you miss these prime opportunities throughout the day?" Janet asked. "I imagine that most of them go unpicked."

"Most do," the Five-Minute Minister admitted. "What ultimately happens as a result of that, only God knows. I'm sure many are wasted, gone forever, like unpicked red tomatoes that rot on the vine. The Book of Jonah shows us that we serve a God of second chances. Unfortunately, the brevity and flow of life do not always allow for second chances. Every ministry opportunity carries with it a unique degree of fruitfulness. Sometimes we never know what transpires after missing an opportunity, or even from responding to one effectively. Running a red light at 5:00 A.M. on Sunday has different ramifications than running a red light at 5:00 P.M. on Friday. Timing is critical. That's why in Ecclesiastes we are told, 'There is a time for everything.' There is a time to work, a time to make money, a time to sleep, and a time to minister. Jesus never ran around frantically, trying to fulfill an appointment schedule. Though he was always unrushed, he was also deliberate, intentional, and therefore incredibly effective and productive. Our constant question as stewards of our God-given lives should be: 'What is the purpose of this moment?' The answer periodically through each day is: 'To minister.'"

For several moments, Tom and Janet sat silently, pondering the Five-Minute Minister's last remarks.

"Why don't more Christians respond to this concept?" Tom asked. "Why have we gone all our lives without ever hearing about these principles?"

"Well, now you see you're a part of the solution, not the problem," the Five-Minute Minister said with a smile. "The main problem here is not lack of knowledge, but lack of obedience. If our obedience quotient came even close to our knowledge quotient, the growth of the church would be unstoppable. It's a matter of the will. Remember when the rich man came and asked Jesus how he could inherit the kingdom of God?"

"Sure," Tom answered. "Jesus said to obey the commandments, which the man claimed he had done, and then he told him to go and sell all he had and give it to the poor."

"Right," the Five-Minute Minister responded. "And it says the man walked away sad, because he was wealthy. Jesus knew that man didn't have a money problem—he had a heart problem. People say, 'If I had more time, I'd do more ministry,' or 'If I had more money, I'd help more people,' or 'If I had more talent, I'd serve God.' You see, it's the same old problem. We don't need more resources to serve God. We need more heart. When Jesus asked Peter three times if he loved him, Peter said yes, but then Jesus told him to *do* something to put his words into action. He was telling Peter, 'You say you love me, but talk is cheap. If you love me, minister to my people.' Ministry is little more than how we demonstrate our love for Christ. When you develop a passion for God, you want to see a fruitfulness in your life."

The Five-Minute Minister deliberated a moment before adding, "I see some exciting trends on the horizon. There is a great host of people like you two who are changing their self-images as Christians and realizing that they can make a difference by practicing their faith on a daily basis. They understand that Jesus did not come into the world just to rearrange their own lives, but to bring transformation to all its people. So they look at life as an adventure, a mission with a noble purpose. All this happens when we tune the desires of our hearts to God's will."

"I think you hit the nail on the head," Tom replied quietly.

"When the leader of a meeting says, 'Take five,' or the director of a movie says, 'Take five,' everyone knows they are to interrupt what they are doing and do something else—to take a break. We need to learn to 'take five' while at work, out to eat, in the stores, at home, so we can respond to God's call to ministry. All of us have to give an account to God some day. On judgment day, there won't be two lines for Christians: clergy and laity. There will be only one line: ministers of God's Word. And those of us who 'took five' on a daily basis will hear the Master say, 'Well done thou good and faithful servant. Come and join the celebration.' Janet and Tom, I think God will use you greatly. He believes in you, and so do I."

The trio closed with prayer. As they stood and hugged their good-byes, the doorbell rang.

The Five-Minute Minister looked at his watch. "I wonder who that could be?" he said, walking to open the front door. There stood a man and woman on the doorstep.

"Hi, we're really sorry to bother you at this late hour," the man said. "I'm Peter, and this is my wife, Jill. Tom and Janet invited us to a Bible study here, but we got home late from work and then got lost on the way over. We were about to drive away when we saw our friends' car in front, so we took a shot at someone's still being here."

"Hey, Peter, Jill," Tom greeted enthusiastically. "Great seeing you."

"Glad you made it," Janet added. "We were wondering what happened to you."

"I'm sorry, everyone," Jill said. "I told Peter it was too late to drop by, but when we saw your car in the driveway, we thought we'd at least let you know we tried to follow up on your invitation."

"Oh, no problem at all, but we were just leaving," Tom offered. "Peter and Jill are new friends of ours. They moved here recently from out of state, and our sons are on the same soccer team," he explained to the Five-Minute Minister.

"That's right," Peter continued. "We were so impressed with Tom and Janet's friendliness and their positive attitude during and after the games that we struck up a conversation one day, which eventually turned into an invitation to visit their church."

"We haven't been to church in years. We really enjoyed last Sunday," Jill added with a smile.

"They are neat people," Janet said, looking at the couple at the door and then toward the Five-Minute Minister. "Oh, I'm so sorry! Peter, Jill, this is—well, we have come to refer to him as the Five-Minute Minister."

The Five-Minute Minister smiled with the same slightly embarrassed grin he had given the first time Ron introduced him to Tom and Janet. Then he responded, "It's nice to meet you."

The secret ingredient in five-minute ministry is having a heart tuned to God's will and being ready and available to be used by him as a positive influence on others.

"The Five-Minute Minister?" Peter inquired.

"They'll explain it to you, I'm sure," the Five-Minute Minister remarked.

"I thought that's what *you* did," Tom commented.

"It's your turn now. It's obvious you two have learned what this is all about," their host said, smiling encouragement at Tom and Janet.

"Come on," Tom said to Peter and Jill, stepping outside, "we'll talk about it over coffee, our treat."

"Good meeting you," Peter and Jill chimed together.

"The pleasure was mine," said the Five-Minute Minister. "Come back next week. The group will be here again, same time."

Just outside the front door, Janet turned and said to him, "You know that person you asked us to think about, someone we admired and looked up to? I was thinking of *you!* Thanks!"

For Reflection and Discussion

1. Have you used any of the power principles of five-minute ministry since you began reading this book? Which ones did you use, and in what ways?

2. What ideas have been most helpful to you in under-standing the concept of "the priesthood of all believers."

For speaking engagements or Five-Minute Ministry training seminars contact the author at the following address:

Alan Nelson
25991 Pala
Mission Viejo, CA 92691

This book is right on. God is going to use it. Practical, incisive, life-related and challenging are the words that describe Alan Nelson's book. It has the potential of unleashing the lay community to discover and utilize their own gifts as ministers in their own right. Such ministry takes place when Jesus is demonstrated to others. Ministry, according to Nelson, is usually like a pinch of salt, a short encounter, a five-minute opportunity to relate. Wrapping his book around ten single principles, the author has put together a book I believe has the potential of releasing thousands to new levels of ministry effectiveness. I highly recommend it for your consideration.

Joe Alrich
president of Multnomah School of the Bible
author of *Lifestyle Evangelism*

While Martin Luther restored the biblical principle of the priesthood of all believers, he never pushed beyond that to the ministry of all believers. Alan Nelson not only affirms the theory of the ministry of all believers, but in *Five Minute Ministry* he shows how it can actually be done even by new and inexperienced church members. Nelson gives us a simple concept with potentially powerful ramifications for church life and growth.

Dr. C. Peter Wagner
professor of church growth, Fuller Seminary

Alan Nelson is one of the most creative pastors I know. This book is the dynamite you can use to explode the myths about "ministry" in your church. If you are a pastor looking for ways to turn your members into ministers, get this book into their hands!

Rick Warren
pastor of Saddleback Valley Community Church

I found *Five Minute Ministry* to be unique and fun to read. The material is presented in a catchy, warm, relational way that captivates the reader. Being a pastor of a meta-church model that is committed to sharing and developing lay people in ministry, I found this book to be right on target. It gives every lay person handles that they can get ahold of in their world of relationships that will communicate Christ's love and make a difference. In fact, as I read the book I was given some very practical principles on ministering through our relationships that I am going to teach my 525 lay pastors who lead the ministry of New Hope Community Church.

Dale Galloway
pastor of New Hope Community Church

In a complex world of growing options vying for our attention, and in a society whose inflationary value of time persuades us to reduce our priority to ministry as lay people, we as the church must hold firm to our commitment to fulfill God's call for each believer. I wholeheartedly teach the Scriptures that tell us that all Christians are to be serving Christ wherever they find themselves. We are all to be active players on God's team. That is why I am excited about Alan Nelson's creative and practical Five Minute Ministry concept. It's a timely idea about making the most of our everday experiences and as a result reaping the fulfillment of making a difference with our lives.

Dr. John C. Maxwell
pastor of Skyline Wesleyan Church
author of *Developing the Leader Within You*

This book's practical teaching on contemporary lifestyle evangelism rings through loud and clear thanks to the tightly-packed examples throughout. Most importantly, Alan Nelson's thesis of being able to equip lay persons to do effective outreach in short shots is both compelling and very marketable! There is nothing out there like it. It meets a tremendous need for simple, concrete, and transferrable training on witnessing. This is a book I heartily recommend, and one I plan to use personally as an evangelism text at the local church level.

Dr. Daniel Reeves
president, Church Consultants Group

If one-half of American pastors and one-quarter of lay leaders would put just ten percent of the principles of Alan Nelson's book into practice, we'd see a 200 percent explosion of the church!

Keith Drury
general director of Local Church Education for the Wesleyan Church

This book clearly shows how readers can easily develop a ministry in their own world, through simple techniques that can produce eternal results. It's an excellent teaching tool for groups and individual study. Put to action, these power principles can produce miraculous results in communities around the world.

Bookstore Journal